This book is dedicated to my mother
Tasikirat Adunni Adewummi-Kareem

Acknowledgements

In the name of Allah, the Most Beneficent, the Most Merciful.

❑ My mother-Alhaja Tasikirat Adewummi-Kareem

I would like to give the greatest thanks to my mother without whose hard work, determination and sacrifice this book would not have been possible. You did one of the hardest things a mother could do for the benefit of her children. Throughout my life, you have been not only my mother, you have been my best friend. You have always been there for us all, you gave me the strength to achieve all I have done and have always pushed me to be the best person I can be. You taught me how to show kindness, humility and respect. You laughter has brought me joy on countless occasions and strength that made me believe I could achieve anything I wanted in life. Thank you.

❑ My father-Alhaji Olanrewaju Kareem

Thank you for your guidance and wisdom over the years. You have made me the man I am today. You taught me how to be independent, gave me principles and nurtured my beliefs. The sacrifices you have made will always be appreciated and will never be forgotten.

❑ My sister-Morufat 'Bolanle Kareem-Omorogbe*

Thanks for the support you have given me my whole life; you set the standards which I always aimed to emulate. I admire your strength and value your leadership. You have been a fantastic older sister and I am grateful for the input you had in making me the man I am today. You always gave me the fuel I needed at crucial points in my life and the belief you showed in me gave me the strength to complete this book. Thank you.

❑ My brother-Moruf Kareem*

You have been there since I began writing this book; thank you for the advice and encouragement you provided. I am always inspired by your positive and enjoyable outlook on life. You have been a great big brother, you gave me protection and advice whenever I have needed it and have always been there for me. Some of the most joyful moments of my life have come from you making me laugh. Thank you.

❑ My sister-Karimot Kareem*

I am proud of the woman you have become; I used to lookout for you but now you look after me. When I told you I was writing a book you said: 'I always knew you would do something like that'. The belief you showed in me brought tears to my eyes. I truly admire your determination and forthrightness. Thank you for your love and support through out my life. Thank you.

❑ My Earth Angel-Mary Iseghohi*

You have been there since the first chapter. I could not have written this book without your tremendous support, advice, encouragement and love. During the most difficult days, you gave me the belief to continue and you did not let me give up. I cherish your love, warmth and kindness and admire your determination and spirit. Thank you.

❑ My brother-Samuel Segun Onabajo*

'I can see you doing something great'. You made this statement before you found out was writing this book. You have shown unwavering faith and support throughout this process; this is testament to the kindness and softness in your heart. You are my 1st big brother and you have always performed your duties stupendously. Thank you for your endless words of encouragement and belief.

❑ My brother-Patrick Omorogbe

Thank you for the support and words of encouragement since you joined the family and marrying my sis and producing my beautiful nephew and niece who have brought so much inspiration into my life. You have been an amazing father, husband, brother and son to members of my family and this is just to say thanks for been always there.

❑ My nephew and niece- Ehizogie and Oluwaseun Omorogbe

I love you both more than I could ever express. You have been my inspiration since you were born and during this process. I love your innocence and truly appreciate the lifetime's worth of joy and happiness you have brought me in just a few short years. Thank you.

❑ Oghenetega Onojeghuo*

Uncle T, you demonstrated the depth of our friendship when I told you I was writing my memoirs. You showed a tremendous amount of patience and provided me with creative inspiration during my many periods of writer's block. You helped shape a number elements of this book. Thank you for your words of encouragement and support, it was truly appreciated.

❑ My Best Friends

Phillip Nyarko, James 'Big' Martey, Olanrewaju Olayemi*, Kabir Adiro, John Oduntoyo, Damilola Ogudenyi, Hursh Shah, Alex Iseghohi*, Amanze Knewke, Fayekemi Adeyemi. From boyhood to manhood, you have been my friends, my confidants, my mentors and my inspiration. You have been there through the laughter and the tears, the good times and bad, have supported me during my most difficult moments and praised me during my highest. I truly appreciate the time I have spent with all of you and I hope you appreciate my friendship as much as I have done yours.

❑ Family and Friends

The Kareem Family; The Adewummi Family; The Adeleye Family, The Adiro Family, The Omorogbe Family, The Adeyemi Family, The Okanla Family; The Sokoya Family, The Iseghohi Family, The Alawode Family, The Bello Family, The Onasile Family, The Milroy Family, The Sumola Family.

Mrs Yemisi Adunni Onabajo, Toyin Oseni, , Sherifat Adiro, Ola Adiro, Rukayat Adiro, Zynab Adiro, Moruf Taiwo Adiro, Morufat Kehinde Adiro, Alhaji Teju Kareem*, Sekinat Taiwo Kareem, Mellisa Milroy-Onabajo*, Ife Kareem, Fola Kareem, Fumbi Kareem, Yinka Onosile, Mrs Nurat Akinola and Family, Mrs Alhaja Bimpe Adeosun-King, Mrs Lawal, Mrs Mariam Moshood and Family, Mrs Savage, Mrs Biola Olusumade, Mrs Iyabo Grifiths, Biyi Alatiba, Dorothy Iseghohi, Gloria Isehoghi, Esther George, Peter Twiddle, Dorota Chojecki*, *Yinka Aileru*, *Janette Weston*, Elena Noe*, Stephen Oquendo, Edwin Gyambibi, Kino Nyarko, Olu Okunnu, Festus Okorie, Tony Jean-Jaques, Sharon Tsang, Pauline Hyman, Jumadin Salumat, Imran Ranian, Karim Salah, Zac Dorkins, Amy Fode, Ife Egwuatu, Neenah Agyapong, Laura Murrell, David de Borja, Tunji Ogunjimi, Kieron Reid, Deborah Oduntoyo, Oduntoyo, Ilaria Dal Pezzo, Steve Wilikinson, Micheal Weller, John Sturman, Louise Hodgson, Valerie Peacock, Nathan Smith, Kabita Begum, Rob Tozer, Sonal Haria, Mike Jones, Jeffery Caron, Steven Mahon.

All my friends and teachers at Omolewa Nursery and Primary School; Christ Church Bentick Primary School,

St Augustine's Secondary School, Hammersmith and Westminster College, and Middlesex University.

R.I.P My Grandparents
Alhaji Khalifat Karimu Bello
Alhaja Ashiwu Bello Adeleye
Alhaji Ashimiyu Bolaji Adewummi
Alhaja Falilat Motolani Aduke Adewummi

*Special thank you for you assistance, belief and support during this process.

Content Page

Foreword

I have known Kabir Kareem-Bello (I call him Kay) from the days when 'men were babies' ... if you know what I mean. My first vivid memory of him was as a stocky two year old running around the house, with snot dripping from his nose and his knickers barely hanging on to his waist. He was the youngest in his family at the time, and I ... I was the older cousin who came over to play on some weekends. That was thirty-something years ago in the ancient city of Ibadan in Nigeria.

Since then, we have both gone on to pursue our different dreams and aspirations, with failures and successes along the way. At the same time, we have also shared many memories together: celebrating birthdays, Christmas and Sallah; saying goodbye in January 1992 when his family was relocating to England; being the one to meet me at the Heathrow Airport on a cold first day of the year in 2005 when I arrived for my postgraduate studies, and ironically, the one that helped packed me up 5 years later when I left; watching Arsenal Football Club matches at the Emirates Stadium (the team we are both passionate about); and, him playing an important role at my wedding by being a groomsman.

In Kay, I have found a man that I have grown to respect a lot. Quiet. Not shy. Personable. Genuine. Dedicated. Intelligent ... very intelligent. And, socially conscious. Perhaps his most endearing quality is his ability to give of himself completely ... both to those who deserve it and those who don't. He has a passionate love for his native country and his allegiance to the Queen is unquestionable. Both countries are indeed home.

A young brilliant writer, his memoir typifies our own generation's experience growing up in a middle-class family in Nigeria in the booming 70s and early 80s and later in the economic decline of the late 80s and 90s, as well as emphasizes the unique and shocking experience of transitioning into a different culture in a more advance country like England. With a skilful narration that is structured according to themes instead of a strict chronological order of events, this memoir wittingly compares life in two different 'worlds' and paints pictures of self discoveries.

Is this book going to enlighten you? Yes. Is it going to make you laugh hard? That is a big YES. Is it going to inspire you? Most definitely! But, even much more, this book iṣ going to transport you through the rich mind fields of a young African in Diaspora.

Samuel Olusegun Onabajo
August 2012

Working on my memoirs December 2011

Prologue

I had been mulling over the idea of writing a book since 2004. The moment the idea was put in my head it seemed insignificant but I could not get it out once it was formulated. I was with a friend of mine at work one afternoon and I began telling him a story about something that happened to me in primary school when I first arrived in England from Nigeria. By the time I finished, he was laughing so hard, tears began to stream from his eyes. I told him I had plenty of stories like that and he suggested I write some of them down.

I didn't actually begin writing any stories until the middle of 2007 as my 30th birthday and the 20th anniversary of my arrival in England loomed ever closer. I began to reflect on my accomplishments, my regrets, moments of happiness, and plans for the future. My intention was to write approximately ten to 15 short anecdotes of some of my exploits following my arrival in England from Nigeria and then share them with just my family and some friends.

I planned to do this as a part-time hobby, something to do when I was bored. It turned out to be the hardest thing I have ever done in my life. Fifteen stories turned to

20, 20 turned to 30. Before I realised it, it had turned into a full-blown project which forced me to dig deep into resources that I didn't know I had. The process of writing these memoirs has been a joyful one but there were some days when I wanted to give up and just put the whole thing away. I could not understand how a hobby which was supposed to take a few months had turned into a beast which consumed five years of my life.

It has been a long and sometimes arduous process, but ultimately it has been one of the most fulfilling things I have ever done. There is one story which I wrote in 20 minutes and there is another which took me the best part of six months to complete. There were occasions when I would write like a man possessed and other days when I would just stare at my laptop for hours on end without writing a single sentence. I would not have been able to complete this book without the help and support of some very special people, my family and friends. I truly appreciate your support; you know who you are.

I will always remember my last day at secondary school as one of the most special days of my life. I was 16 years old and had been in England for just over five years. I was about to start a new chapter of my life and I felt totally unprepared for what was ahead. As I wondered what the future held in store for me, I looked back at the significant moments which had shaped who I was up till that point in my life. This book is a compilation of some of my memories from that day.

It was a hot summer's day in June 1997, the sun was shinning and I was sitting on a bench in the school garden with seven of my school friends. We had just attended our last official lesson as Year 11 students and would soon be taking our GCSE exams. Nostalgia was in the air; most of us had known each other for five years. The majority of us met in September 1992 as excited and frightened young boys and girls; now we were teenagers. I had spent the best five years of my life at the school where I experienced great joys and deep sadness. I made friends and enemies: some enemies became friends but not a single friend became an enemy. There had been laughter and tears, fights won and lost, love and heartbreak.

Before settling down on the benches, we had spent the previous couple of hours laughing, reminiscing and swapping stories about our experiences. Most of the morning was spent signing each other's shirts as we had seen the seniors doing the previous year, taking pictures and putting messages in our friends' notebooks. A politician named Ken Livingstone had been the guest speaker at our last assembly the day before. A piece of career advice he gave was to learn Chinese because China was projected to be the biggest economy in the next 20 years. (How I wish I had taken heed of that advice). We had also attended a careers' fair the week before; it was meant give us information about the choices available to us and the next steps to take after secondary school, but it just made me realise I didn't have a clue about what I wanted to do in the future.

As I sat watching my friends, I wondered if they were experiencing the same feelings as me. I was a little scared of what I would face once I had left what had become my sanctuary. I thought to myself: have I made lifelong friends or will we go our separate ways? Will I do well in my GCSE exams if I study hard enough? Will I go to Sixth Form here or go to college? Am I bright and determined enough to go to University? What job will

I be qualified to do? Will I make my parents proud of me? A thousand questions seemed to be racing through my mind at once and I didn't have an answer or plan for most of them. I had been looking forward to that day for so long but when it actually arrived I desperately wished I had more time.

With each that minute passed, I became more petrified thinking about what the future held, I saw a little black boy running towards where I was sitting. He reminded me so much of myself when I had started secondary school five years earlier. This was the catalyst for my trip down memory lane. Allow me to introduce myself, my name is Kabir Kareem and I've got some stories to tell. I remembered...

Where it all began

... The earliest memories of my childhood in the late Eighties were filled with joy and happiness. I was born in the city of Ibadan in Nigeria to Mr Olanrewaju and Mrs Tasikirat Adunni Kareem who were both educated professionals. My mother was a nurse who worked in one of the biggest hospitals in the country: University College Hospital in Ibadan. My father was the accountant for a multinational company called Leyland. I am the third of four children: Morufat is the first-born, Moruf is second and Karimot is the last.

I would describe our social standing as middle-class; my well-travelled parents were members of a number of exclusive social clubs. We went to the Ibadan country club at least two weekends a month. The parents would sit by the bar and be served by waiters while us children would play in a huge adventure playground or go swimming in the pool. The economy was booming which was supported by a strong middle class and the Naira was on par with the pound sterling. My parents would reminisce years later about the good times by saying `I remember when ₦1 was equal to £1`. The first place I recall living was in a gated community called The

Village. It was specifically built for the employees of Leyland and it was the period of my life I most associate with luxurious living. All house guests had to announce themselves at the security gate before gaining entry. There was a small park and there was small lake with dolphins in it. Electricity rationing was rife but when NEPA (National Electrical Power Authority) took away the electric power, we would have full power within five minutes from our own generator while the rest of the city would be without for hours or even days. We were driven to and from school in the company Land Rover, sometime our dad took us in his own Range Rover. The crown jewel of The Village was the swimming pool located within the compound.

Basically, life was very good. Suddenly, however, over what seemed like a very short period of time, people began to move out of The Village. As children, we didn't understand why. We moved into a three bedroom flat in Akobo and we stopped going to the country club. It would not be until years later, when talking to my parents, would I understand the realities of life after we moved out of The Village. My dad had been made redundant, as had others in The Village, the economy was going downhill, and basic goods had become scarce and expensive. Corruption and the Structural Adjustment Programme (SAP) had made life difficult and the horizon, at that time, had looked bleak.

As tough as things had become, my parents worked hard to ensure that it did not affect us children. Food was always available. With two cars, a chauffeur and a housemaid, we lived a comfortable and privileged life compared to some of my school friends, some of whom I had seen selling oranges to passing cars after school.

My dad went into the farming business; he raised and sold poultry, and also owned farmland which was used to grow tomato and spinach. Some of my most cherished childhood memories were of me and my siblings going to help my dad plant seeds on the farm. He became known in the neighbourhood as '*Alhaji Ele-fo' (Alhaji the vegetable farmer)*. My mum said that for sake of her children, at that time she began to contemplate working abroad like some of her colleagues. Six months after moving to Akobo, we moved into a house my parents had been building. It was not finished but would be a duplex when fully completed a few years later. My mum recently told me that seeing the joy on my face on the day we moved in - and me saying to her 'mummy, this is our house' - strengthened her desire give us a better life. At that moment, she made a decision which broke her heart; she would start making plans to go and work abroad. In 1988 she left to work in Saudi Arabia as a nurse for approximately 18 months. She returned to Nigeria for a few months after the contract ended, then went to work in London. (I will always be thankful for her sacrifice). We all missed her so much. The only thing that made her time away from us bearable was the hope and belief that we would soon join her in London.

I had missed her so much on my tenth birthday that I prayed that she would be around for my eleventh. I will always remember the day my mum returned from London as being one of the most joyful days of my life. It was a normal morning - I was having one of my many squabbles with my little sister - when I saw our orange Volkswagen Beetle drive through the gate. I saw my dad step out of the car and yell, '*mummy ti de o*'. I could not believe my eyes when I saw the person stepping out of the passenger side was my mother. I shrieked '*mummmmy ti de', mummmmy ti de*', then jumped over the balcony railing in one swift movement and ran towards the car. The sprint to the car lasted barely thirty seconds, but the closer I got, the further she seemed. I refused to believe I was not dreaming until I touched her, so I jumped on her with such force that she actually fell back into the car. Barely five seconds later, Moruf and Karimot had piled on top of her as well.

It was the single greatest moment of my short ten years. I had missed her smooth skin, her warmth and her laughter, and I was now so happy I began to cry. My dad had gone to pick her up at the airport without telling us. I held her hand all the way into the house because I was afraid that if I let her go she would disappear. When she settled down in the living room, I kept on touching her face and pulling her cheeks just to make sure that she wasn't a mirage. Throughout that day, I spent every single moment I could with her, and I futilely fought my desire to sleep that night just in case she disappeared. When I woke up the next morning, the first thing I did was to go to my parents' bedroom to check that she was there. My eleventh birthday was the greatest day of my life, not only because my mum was with us but it had been confirmed that we would be going to live in London.

The Journey Begins

... My dad was a man who liked to do things in secret. Even before my mum came back, I got a feeling we might be leaving Nigeria because my father, when watching the news, often said 'I am tired of this country, I am tired, I can't wait to leave'. After much discussion with my siblings, we all came to the conclusion that we were definitely going to live in London. I don't actually remember being told that we were coming to London, I think we just went along with the flow. In the two months before we left, we went to see our family friends and travelled to Lagos to collect our visas. As a ten year-old this was probably the best period of my life so far. The excitement in the house during that period was palpable.

On 11th January 1992, we were due to leave for London the next day. My mum had bought me some brand new shoes, new clothes and a gold chain. My dad had had arranged for my uncle to drive us to the airport and he was supposed to have arrived around 4pm in the afternoon. I started to panic when he had not arrived by 6pm, but by 8pm I was close to tears. I started to get the 'I knew it was too good to be true' feeling. The house, which had been bubbly and full of life few hours previously, had become deadly silent. (I recently asked Morufat how she felt during this period. She said she thought to herself: 'the devil is liar') My dad was fuming and my mum tried to calm him down by reassuringly saying, 'don't worry, he will soon arrive'. I went and sat by the window in my parent's bedroom and stared at the front gate. I sat there for a good two hours until it got dark. My heart jumped with hope every time I heard a car horn or saw a headlight near our gate. My hopes were dashed each time. I felt my dream was being destroyed with each passing minute, so I began to pray.

At 9pm, my dad decided we would have take taxis to an airport hotel because it didn't look like my uncle was going to arrive. At around 9:30pm, I finally saw the headlights from the van at the front gates. The relief that washed over me then was indescribable. My uncle received a tongue-lashing from my dad, and he made up some silly excuse about a hold-up on the express. He was my favourite uncle, but for a few minutes then I wanted to slap him silly. We began to load the suitcases into the van. Everything that could be packed had been packed, from clothes and shoes to the cooking utensils used to make *eba* and *amala*. These are the staple foods of Nigeria and are described as solids. *Eba* is made from cassava, and *amala* is made from dried yam which is then ground into flour. My favourite food was *eba* with my mother's *egusi* soup.

As I lay in my bed that night, I imagined how London was going to look. I imagined it being covered thick snow and I would stand out as the only black boy walking in the streets full of white people. While drifting off to sleep, I pictured my family living just like the Huxtables from *The Cosby Show*, only we would be in London.

When I woke up the on the morning of 12th January 1992, it felt like I had only closed my eyes for a few seconds. When I finished getting dressed, I went into every room in the house to say goodbye, then walked around the outside of the house. A single tear rolled down my right cheek as I remembered all the great memories I had of living there. When it was time to leave, my dad gathered the family in the foyer and said a short prayer. As we drove through the gates, I looked back at the house I had lived in most of my life for the last time; I didn't know how long it would be before I saw it again. My journey from Akobo to London had begun.

During the drive to the airport, we were all very excited but quiet. I prayed that the journey to the airport would be incident-free. It would be the wrong time to have a flat tire. When we arrived at the airport, I looked admiringly at the famous Muritala Muhammad Airport, which was as grand as I had always imagined. As we got out of the van, some porters rushed towards us and began to unload our approximately twenty pieces of luggage. I felt like the elite of the elite. Inside the airport, my dad went off to get our tickets while the rest of us stayed with my mum. While waiting, I suddenly saw my Aunty Sheri and my cousins and we rushed to hug them. After the initial greetings, Aunty Sheri told my mum that one of her sisters-in-law died during childbirth earlier that morning. This was the first time I had seen my mother cry and it was heartbreaking to watch. Selfishly I thought about myself. I thought, 'I won't be going to London, I won't get to go on a plane, and I'll have to go back to that bloody school'. My dad came back and said he had got the tickets and I felt so relieved, even though he looked like he had just been in a fight. Morufat told me years later that the reason my dad looked so upset was that he had nearly come to blows with airport officials because they asked him for bribes. They saw that he was taking his four children to London and assumed that he was rich. My dad has always been a man of principle and he refused to pay any bribes, so they made things as difficult for him as they could. Looking back now, I realise how single-minded I had been. My mum was crying, someone had just died, and all I could think about was London.

While we were waiting to go to the departures area, I went to use the toilet. Entering a stall, I did my business and then tried to unlock the door. Although I had just finished doing a 'number 2', I nearly did a panicky number 2 again because I could not unlock the door. It was stuck. I started to cry because I really believed my family were going to get on the plane and leave me in this country. Luckily for me, my cousin Kabir came to use the toilet and with a bit of pushing and pulling we managed to pry the door open. The relief I felt was twice what I felt when I saw my uncle's headlights then night before. I had been stuck in there for at least five minutes and those were the longest five minutes of my life.

Everyone, except my dad, began to cry as we said goodbye to Aunty Sheri and my cousins. It was not until that moment that I realised the magnitude of what I would be leaving behind: my family, my friends and my home.

The Plane

... I was almost as excited about getting on the plane as actually going to London. My siblings and I had never been on a plane before so we were all very excited. Morufat walked with the suave manner of a frequent flyer but I knew she was as excited as I was. My mum had to go downstairs to the tarmac to identify our luggage. This was part of the security check or else they would not have been loaded onto the plane. I thought to myself, 'What kind of backwards system is this?'

The wait in the departure lounge was long and boring. My mum told me that the plane was late, and I only later came to understand that this was the norm. As far back as I could remember, I had always dreamed about how I was going to enter a plane. I had thought about this since the day I was told we were going to London. Like I had seen countless times on TV, I would walk across the tarmac and the plane would be so close I would be able to touch it. I would then walk up the stairs, give a last wave and then enter the plane.

When it was actually time to board, we walked through a tunnel which I thought would lead to the tarmac, and then we would walk the short distance to the plane. Suddenly I saw some stewardess and what looked like the entrance to the plane. My dream had been cruelly shattered. This was not at all how I imagined this moment, and I realised I wouldn't get to see the plane that was taking me to London up close. I wouldn't be walking up those stairs and there would be no waving. This would be the first of many disappointments. I wanted to be the first of my siblings to enter a plane; I mean this only happens once and I would hold the bragging rights for life. Unfortunately my mum and Karimot were walking ahead of my dad and I. Nothing seemed to be going to plan; firstly no stairs, now Karimot was going to enter the plane before me. I will never forget what happened next for the rest of my life: I rushed forward, nudged Karimot out of the way and extended my right foot as far as it would go onto the plane. I did all this just to say I was the first of my siblings to set foot on a plane and I don't regret it one bit.

I got over my disappointment as soon I got onto the plane, it was all like I imagined and seen on television. The seats, the seat belts, the aisles, the overhead storage and, best of all, the cinema screen. My dad pointed to a seat and told me to sit down. Out of sheer excitement I buckled my seatbelt as soon as my bum hit the seat. He then told me that I was sitting in the wrong seat and I should move one seat over. Putting the seatbelt on was easy, but taking it off was difficult. I had no idea how I was supposed to take it off and I thought I was going to get into trouble for putting my seatbelt before I was told to. My dad saw that I was struggling and with one swift flick, he had unbuckled it.

We didn't all sit together, Moruf and I sat with my dad in the middle of the plane, Karimot sat with my mum by the window seats and Morufat sat by herself on the window seat. We sat on the plane, which didn't seem to be going anywhere, for what seemed like eternity. I started to get that 'it was too good be true feeling' again. I kept thinking something was going to go wrong which wouldn't allow us to fly. Maybe the plane didn't have enough petrol or the pilot didn't turn up for work?

After an hour-and-a-half of waiting idly on the tarmac, the plane started to move. It kept moving on the ground for what felt like hours. I prayed that nothing would go wrong or that the airline hadn't left someone behind so we would have to go back. Then it started to speed up and shake, the engines began to roar and I felt weightless for a few seconds as it lifted off the ground. This was it, my date with destiny had arrived. Next stop, London.

Dream Fulfilled

… The plane journey was uneventful. I walked up and down the aisles as much as I could when my dad was asleep. I didn't really sleep much because I kept dreaming that my journey was a dream which caused me to wake up. There was one last disappointment the journey had in store for me. I had never been to a cinema before and I very excited about the prospect of watching a movie on the plane. True to form for this particular airline, the screen did not work.

The announcement came over the PA system to tell us that, because of bad weather and the late departure of the plane, we would not be landing at Heathrow airport. The plane had been diverted to Gatwick. I distinctly remember my dad saying, 'oh blast'. I was not at all bothered. As long as we landed in England, I didn't really care at which airport. The plane started to descend approximately an hour after the pilot's announcement. It got lower and lower and suddenly there was an almighty jolt. I was so scared, I thought the plane was going to crash. I turned to look at my dad and he looked as calm as a summer sea, then I knew that everything would be fine.

When the plane finally came to a standstill, there was a sudden commotion as people got their bags from the overhead lockers in a hurry to get off the plane. I don't remember which of my siblings got off the plane first and I think I was too tired to rush to be the first to step on English soil. When we got off the plane, we walked into another tunnel, but I was not too disappointed because I was expecting it. I will never forget my first thoughts when we finally got off the plane: 'So now what?'

That was when I began to think about where we were going to live. What school would we be going to go? What job would my dad do? Would we still be able to eat *eba*, *amala* and *asaro*? These questions kept going through my head until we reached the platform to board the tram. We got onto a tram which took us to collect our luggage which took approximately five minutes. In those five minutes I kept looking at each end of the tram looking for the driver. I was amazed when I realised that no one was driving and then I wondered how we were going to stop.

We collected our bags from baggage claim; we were the last there because we had so many bags. I used an escalator for the first time in my life as we made our way to Customs. By the time we got there, I was exhausted and the excitement had begun to diminish. I became more tired as the night wore on. Going through Customs was a blur. I remember seeing a lot of *oyinbo* (white) people and some of the passengers we were on the plane with. I began to feel a little chilly, but I didn't feel the full effect of the cold because of the excitement and adrenaline.

Having landed at Gatwick instead of Heathrow, my mum had to make arrangements to find somebody who would be willing to take six people and twenty pieces of luggage to where we were supposed to be staying. We all waited for about forty-five minutes while my mum looked for some transportation. She finally found a cab which we shared with some other people going our way. My first trip in a car into London is not something I can claim to remember. I entered the van and then woke up in front of a semi-detached house in Hammersmith.

Hammersmith

... Upon arrival, we walked into the warm house belonging to my mum's friend Aunty Bummi. I had met out hosts briefly back home, but I did not know what to expect. I was apprehensive that we wouldn't get along with them or I would do something embarrassing because everything was new. Aunty Bummi was also a nurse and had shared a flat with my mum in London a few years previously. She and her family had made a similar journey as us from Nigeria approximately a year before. She had three kids who were much younger than me and my siblings; the oldest was Damilola and he was the same age as Karimot. He would go on to be one of my best friends over the next few years. My aunt shrieked excitedly when she opened the door and saw us; I tried to prostrate but she grabbed me and gave me a massive hug. She hugged everybody else as well and motioned for us to make our way into the living-room. I was at ease immediately. Shortly after we arrived, my aunt's husband arrived home; he had gone to meet us at Heathrow airport and brought coats for us to wear. An hour after we arrived, I suddenly felt exhausted and all I wanted to do was sleep. Aunty Bummi showed me to a bed which I was to share with Moruf and I fell asleep before my head hit the pillow. I wish I could say that I slept through the night but I kept dreaming that the whole journey had been a dream and I was still in my bed back home.

When I woke up the next morning, the first thing I did was to look around me to confirm that the past twenty-four hours had been real. I eagerly looked into the garden to see if it was snowing, but it wasn't. I did this every morning for a week and was disappointed every time. I began to feel I had been deceived most of my life. I had been told I would see snow, but I did not know then that I would not see my first snowflake for another four years. The ironic thing was that we could not land at Heathrow airport because of heavy snow.

I went downstairs and my family were drinking tea. My dad sat us all down and told us to be grateful and respectful to our host. After a ten minute talk, I went to get breakfast, and this was the first time I had Rice Crispies with fresh milk. It was a horrible experience, and I spat them out as soon as they hit my tastebuds. My dad was sitting right opposite me and I thought he was going to force me to eat. Fortunately he took pity on me and asked Aunty Bummi to make me some bread and egg. Even this tasted different to what I was used to. This was one of many bad food experiences during my time in England. While eating breakfast, I noticed the fireplace which made think of Father Christmas. I had always had my doubts about him from a very young age. He was always supposed to come down a chimney but there were no chimneys in all the Christian houses I had ever been to in Nigeria. My doubts were finally confirmed when I was about seven. I went on a school trip to see Santa but the Santa whose lap I sat on was a skinny black man name Ahmed.

My first few days in London were a combination of boredom and discovery. I was glad that there was electricity available twenty-four hours a day, which took a while to get used to. For the first three days, I would become very restless at around 7pm because I felt that I should be doing something which I wasn't doing. On the third night, I realised the cause of my unease at that particular time. Back home we would get ready for the night ahead by bringing out the torch lights and candles for the inevitable power cuts by NEPA. I don't think that there is company on this earth which has been vilified more than NEPA. Back in Nigeria, there had been countless occasions in which my family and I would be engrossed in a movie and the electricity would suddenly cut out. We would all furiously shout 'NEEPPPPAAAAAAAA!!!!!' Despite all the inconvenience it caused, I believe NEPA was one of the reasons my siblings and I became very close. Without electricity, we couldn't watch television so we played and talked amongst ourselves. Some of my most treasured memories growing up are of sitting on the veranda at night with my brother and sisters looking at the stars. The dark night was pierced by the flame from a single candle or lantern, and the only sounds were of frogs and insects in the bushes which surrounded our house. During the weekends and holidays, all the neighbourhood kids would come out to play during a blackout, but as soon as the electricity came back, everyone would disappear to their houses. We would only come back out when the power was taken again which could be anything from five minutes to five days. We spent most of our time playing outside which forced us to be imaginative and resourceful. Some of my friends created ingenious toys out of seemingly useless objects.

In London television programmes were on from morning till night. Daytime television was extremely boring, but I had no cause to complain. I was accustomed to rationed television watching my whole life. In Nigeria, television programmes did not start before 4pm on a weekday. Even then we were only able to watch TV when there was electricity which was often irregular. I was also amazed at the fact that bottles of milk always appeared outside the front door every morning. It wasn't until a few weeks later that I realised they actually paid for the milk; I thought everybody in England received free milk. Letters were delivered nearly every day which reminded of the thirty minute drive my dad would have to make to the University of Ibadan to check his post-box and retrieve his mail. We didn't really eat a lot of English food apart from sausages, fish fingers and Frosted Flakes cereal.

When the kids went to school, it was extremely boring and the highlight of my day would be when they returned home around 3:45pm. I went along to collect them from school on a couple of occasions and I felt the school looked very odd the first time I saw it. It looked like a very big mansion with playground games painted on the concrete floors and walls. My first impression was that it looked very dull. When the school bell rang, I was amazed at how odd the *oyinbo* kids looked. I had never seen so many in my life and they all looked alike.

Weekends were the most exciting times. I watched more cartoons over my first two weekends than I had ever watched in my whole life. I was also introduced to TV shows such as *Little House on the Prairie*, *Raw Hide* and *Land of the Giants*. These were to become some of my favourite TV shows. Again I felt odd when I woke up on the weekends. In Nigeria, I would be expected to carry out my chores, which included sweeping the sitting rooms, verandas and pavement around the house. None of that was expected from me in England.

Landward Court

… I was so excited when my mum told us that she had got us our own place to live. I enjoyed my time at Hammersmith but it was starting to get a bit claustrophobic. The council had assigned us a three bedroom flat in Edgware Road. When we got off the bus near our block of flats, the first thing I noticed was an imposing building called the Victoria Casino. I didn't know that it was a gambling establishment during the whole period we lived in the area. All I knew was that there was always a doorman outside and people who came there always came in expensive cars.

When we got to the front of our building, which was twelve storeys high, the first thing that struck was the name of the building: 'Landward Court'. To me, it sounded strong and imposing. It would be my home for the next two and a half years. We all got into the lift and went up to the fifth floor. The lift doors opened and I stepped out into a carpeted hall. I was very disappointed when I entered the flat, because it looked nothing like the Huxtable house. There was a hallway with three bedrooms on the right-hand side, the bathroom, toilet and kitchen were on the left and the adjoining living room and dining room were at the far end of the hall. My parents had the biggest bedroom, which was closest to the living room. My sisters had the room next to their's and the boy's room was by the front door. Although I was a little disappointed at the size of the flat, I was very glad we had our own place. My bedroom was pretty small, and this room was meant for a single bed but now had two single beds wedged in it.

By comparison, our house in Nigeria was a mansion and this place was a bedsit. I could walk from one end of the flat to the other in less than twenty steps. The living room was just about big enough to fit a brown three-piece sofa suite, a piece of furniture which I really hated. It was separated from the dining room by a divider which I initially found fascinating but soon got bored with after a while.

The real problem was that I felt the flat lacked character. It had been lived in by countless people before we moved and didn't feel like home. We were the first to live in our house in Nigeria as my parents had designed and built it. In the east wing of the house, there was the kitchen and dining room. In the middle was a living room which was big enough for two three-piece sofa suites, one for the adults and the other side for the kids. A reception area, three bedrooms (one with an ensuite bathroom) and a prayer room. It also had four verandas and a massive compound with a small football pitch.

The only thing I liked about the Landward Court flat was the two bathrooms. My parents decided that the bathroom directly in front of their room would be theirs and the second one would be for the kids. Our bathroom was cream with the toilet and bath in the same place. What caught my eye was the chrome tap with a cradle which the shower head rested perfectly on. The shower head was connected to the tap via a long silver and metallic hose. I had seen this type of shower in a James Bond movie and had always imagined using one like it one day and I couldn't wait to use it. My dad specifically told us not to touch the round silver knob located between the tap heads. Although this bathroom was a lot more user-friendly and modern than what I was used to in Nigeria, and even back there the one we had at home was hi-tech compared to what my cousins used. We always had hot water, indoor plumbing and the comfort to wash in privacy. A lot of my school friends and some cousins had to wash outside or use a shared bathroom with water that had drawn from a well and poured into an oil drum. I got over my initial disappointment about our English flat quickly when I realised how lucky I was. I realised I was with my family in our own place in London, and so I had the best night's sleep since we arrived.

The first breakfast we had has a family will always be one of my most cherished moments of the early days in London. My mum and Morufat made a massive breakfast of eggs, sausages, baked beans, toasts and fish fingers. We all sat around the table and ate our first meal in London as a family.

My Parents, London 1992

My Family, London 1992

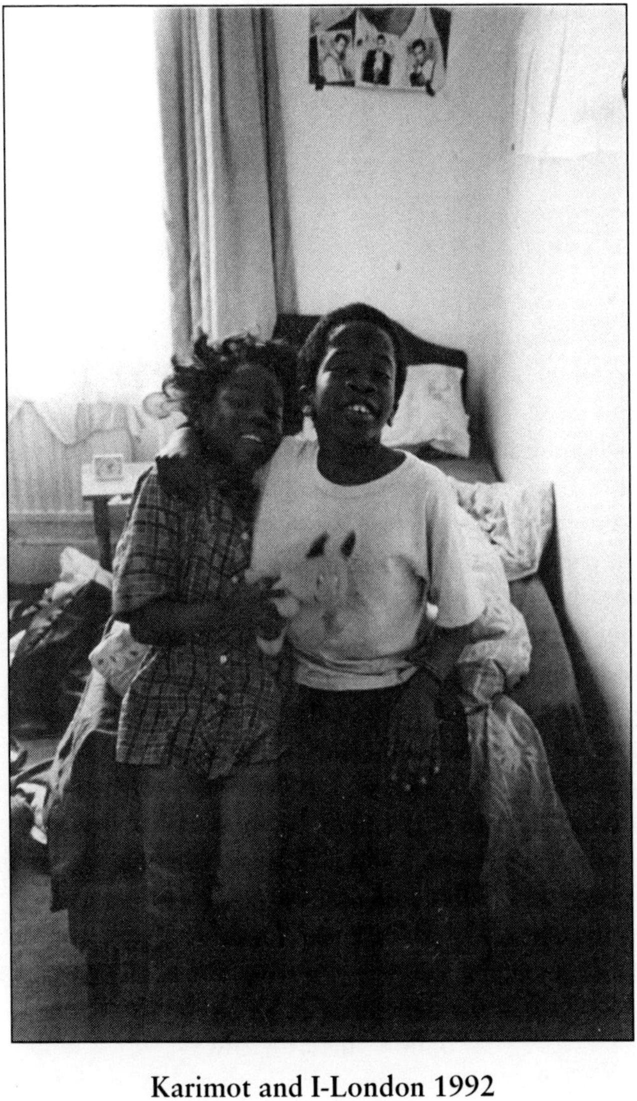

Karimot and I-London 1992

London

... My first few weeks in London were the most exciting period of my life so far. The weather was the most significant difference to Nigeria, it was cold but the air smelt and felt fresh. Sometimes, the aroma reminded me of the times we opened my mum's suitcase when she returned to Nigeria from London. It was almost as if she had packed some of the smell and brought it along with everything else in the suitcase. The novelty soon began to wear off when the cold began to bite. (I will tell you more about that later).

Whilst it was exciting, I also began to think of the sun rays of Nigeria and started to suffer withdrawal symptoms. The skies of London were dull compared to Nigeria, here it got dark by 4pm and it was always cloudy. Back home, I was able to see the blue sky on the average day. What I missed the most was being able to see the stars. My siblings and I used to spend countless evenings on the balcony enjoying the cool breeze and looking up at the dark skies lit up by the stars.

However, in London, there was always something new which I found fascinating or exciting. I was impressed with nearly everything that I saw. Every single road was smooth, and there was not a single pothole in sight. There were no open sewers and no sagging power lines. Walking on the smooth pavements without the discomfort of needing to step out of the way of a car took a little while to get used to. The streets were spotless, the traffic lights worked, and night street lights made it possible to go out without a torch. Although I was expecting to see all of these things, they still fascinated me.

Ironically, seeing how smooth and orderly things were in London made me appreciate the tenacity and ingenuity of my countrymen. I also realised the level of skill and aggression needed to be a driver on Nigerian roads. Back home, the driving was rough and the official road rules were ignored. The majority of cars didn't have indicators that worked, drivers usually put their hands out of the window and waved to show that they were about to turn left or right. The two most important parts of the car which needed to be good working order were the brakes and the horn.

In general, things were very difficult for the average person in Nigeria. The extent of poverty was evident on every street. The lack of electricity made life even more difficult, street sanitation was nonexistent and the crime rate was pretty high. But through all the hardship and pain, people persevered, laughed and hoped for a better tomorrow. Some seemed to thrive in the presence of chaos. The first time I saw a zebra crossing in London, it reminded me of the one which was put on the main road near Akobo. When they finished the zebra crossing on the road, I asked my dad what its purpose was. He told me that cars were meant to stop for people to cross. In the two years before we left Nigeria, I did not see a single car stop for a pedestrian. In fact I believe the unwritten rule for that section of the road was 'cross at your own risk'.

The infrastructure of London was one the things which I found most impressive. Some of the architectural designs of the buildings had a sense of timelessness about them. A lot of the houses, government buildings and museums looked exactly like those in books like *Peter Pan* and *Dick Whittington and His Cat* which I had read as a child. Some of the architectural designs of the building had a sense of timelessness about them. Moreover, every street had a name. I had always found it impressive when my parents gave directions back home, where streets often didn't have names. Three things were always required: the name of the area, a landmark and the description of the place.

After a while I began to miss the noise from cars horns, people interacting on the streets, the hawkers and market traders. I noticed that people in London minded their own business and didn't really interact with each other. One of the experiences which took a little while to get used to was using public transportation. Back home we went everywhere by car. I could count the amount of times I used public transport on one hand, because we lived a very sheltered life. While being driven to school by my parents or the chauffer, I used to look enviously as kids my age or younger than me took public transport to school by themselves. The first time I took public transport in Nigeria was both exciting and scary. I was nine and I begged Moruf to let me follow him to Bashorun market. On the way there he flagged down a taxi which was already filled to capacity but we still managed to squeeze in. We spent about an hour in the market before we went to the bus stop to catch a *danfo* (minibus) home. While waiting, Moruf told me very sternly that I had to be smart or else I would get left behind. Nothing could have prepared me for what happened next. As soon as an empty *danfo* arrived at the bus stop, everybody waiting rushed to get on before it had even come to a full stop. My brother was pulling me so hard that I thought my hand was going fall off. People were pushing and shoving me from all sides. I tried my hardest to push back but I was no match for these seasoned travellers. I lost my right shoe but I still managed to get on. We sat at the back of the bus but because I sat on my brother's lap, the conductor charged us the fee of a single passenger.

Transportation in London was very different. I remember going out with my dad one day and we saw some people waiting at the bus stop. There was an orderly queue with no shouting or shoving. The bus came and everybody got on one at a time. I also saw hundreds of taxis but I still stared at each one like it was the first time. Some carried single passengers while others carried more. This was one of the things which verified I was certainly no longer in Nigeria. Back home, I regularly saw taxis with two people in the front seat, five or six at the back and a ram in the boot.

It felt good being a foreigner in a foreign land. It was the first time I had ever been a tourist and I thoroughly enjoyed it. It felt fantastic to see new things for the first time. I was always excited to go somewhere because it was guaranteed that I would see or experience something new. Two of my most enjoyable adventures were the trips to Oxford Circus and Trafalgar Square.

My first trip to Oxford Street with my mother and Karimot will always remembered as one of the interesting days of my life. My mum told us on the morning of the trip that we were going shopping to buy some new clothes for school. While waiting at the bus stop, I asked my mum which bus we would be taking, she mentioned a few choices. I hoped we would take the bus with the open back or a double decker. I had been itching to take one of these buses since we arrived but all the buses we had taken so far were single deckers. At some point, I believed that my mum did not like the double decker buses which was why we always took the single decker, it was a while before I realised that the buses were numbered for a specific reason. I was so disappointed the first bus to arrive was a single decker. I grudgingly got on the bus, watched my mum pay the bus driver and eagerly tore off the ticket. The journey was short and when we got off, I nearly lost my mum in the sea of people. I had never seen anything like it before in my life. There were hundreds of thousands of people in the longest street I had ever seen. It took a few minutes to gather my bearing. I could not walk in a straight line without having to avoid hitting somebody. There were hundreds of shops on either side of the street, some were small while others were humongous. I was so excited I wanted to go into every single of them.

We followed my mum into a shop called C&A. Apart from the airports, this was the biggest building I had ever been in. It was filled with clothes, and it had escalators and even a restaurant. We were in there for approximately two hours, but I wanted to leave after the first thirty minutes. My mum seemed to look at everything on every rack. I saw what I wanted within the first twenty minutes and was ready to leave. One of the things which I found very bizarre was the fact the price of everything ended in ninety-nine pence. When we finished at C&A, I wanted to cry when my mum said she wanted to go to a few more shops. My initial thrill had disappeared and I just wanted to leave. While walking to the other shops, I became annoyed any time my mum stopped just to look in their windows. She saw us getting restless and said, 'she was window shopping'. This concept made no sense to me. Why was she looking at stuff she was not going to buy? A couple of hours later, I was exhausted and was delighted when my said that we were going to get something to eat. We walked towards Marble Arch and walked into Kentucky Fried Chicken. I will always remember this as the day my love for Kentucky Fried Chicken began. I had never tasted chicken like it before, the succulent meat fell off the bone effortlessly and the skin was delicious.

The Trafalgar Square trip was the most memorable. Aunty Bummi took me, my siblings and her own kids. I loved being a tourist. The simplicity of the landmark itself was one of the things I found most remarkable. I had seen the pigeons on TV but I still stared in total amazement at the amount of birds that were in the square. I wished we had brought bread to feed them like some *oyinbo* people were doing. We took pictures by the water fountains and then by the giant lion statues. I felt like I was on top of the world when we all climbed on the back of the lions to take pictures. After Trafalgar Square, we walked towards the Houses of Parliament. I was stunned when Aunty Bummi pointed towards Downing Street and said that it was where the Prime Minister lived. I could not help being impressed by the accessibility of everything: the Houses of Parliament and Buckingham Palace and Downing Street were all within walking distance.

Trafalgar Square 1992

Morufat, Karimot and I-KFC 1992

Two technological marvels I saw blew my mind. About two weeks after moving into Landward Court, I walked into the middle of a conversation my parents were having. My mum was holding a rectangular piece of plastic and explaining something to my dad who was listening intently. I distinctly remember my mum saying, 'I have my own four numbers which will use to take out money'. My dad looked a little confused and asked, 'what is the number?' My mother replied, 'I can't tell you because I am the only one that can know it, even the bank don't know it'. The whole conversation had become a little too complicated for me to follow and I lost interest.

The conversation made sense to me a day later. Karimot and I were watching TV one Saturday evening and mum asked us if we would like to follow her to the bank. I was very impressed at the fact that banks were open on a Saturday evening. I always enjoyed walks with my mum because every time we walked somewhere it was always an adventure. During the ten minute walk I recalled our visits to the bank in Nigeria. Mum or dad would pick us up from school and drive to the Union Bank on the site of the hospital where she worked. She would park the car outside and tell us to behave ourselves whilst she went in. She usually spent approximate thirty to forty minutes in there. I always imagined that the inside of a bank would be one of the coolest places ever. I imagined a dimly lit room with green lights. People would enter, wait a few minutes and then a finely dressed banker would call them into a private room to give the money you needed. I could never understand why my parents walked out of the bank looking stressed. I guess I should have known that getting money out of the bank would never be so simple in Nigeria. Although

I hated waiting the car, I always felt privileged because only people with lots of money would need to put their money into a bank. Only poor or uncivilised people continued to hide their money under their mattresses or money belts like the market traders.

Back in London, we were walking towards the Halifax bank and I asked my mum if that was the bank we were going to. When she confirmed that it was, I burst into a spontaneous run. Finally after eleven years I was about to enter a bank. The sprint only lasted a couple of minutes, but in that short period I let my imagination run wild. I pictured the inside of the bank as like the ones I had seen in advertisements. I was disappointed when I got to the front door and found it locked. My disappointment was soon replaced by sheer amazement when I saw what happened next. I waited for my mum and sister to meet me by the door, but my mum went towards a machine which was inside the wall. I had walked past this particular machine a couple of times before but did not have a clue what it was for. Curiosity forced me to walk towards where they were standing to see how this thing worked. I watched my mum take out the plastic rectangle from her purse and put it into the machine. What happened next will stay with me for the rest of my life. She pressed some numbers on the machine but nothing happened. Then she pressed more numbers, still nothing happened. All of the sudden the machine began to make noise and then produced money. I must have been staring at the machine in amazement because when I next looked at my mum, she had a smile on her face. I would like to think I had brought her joy at that moment because of my look of total amazement.

The outdoor toilet was a futuristic-looking contraption that reminded me of one of my favourite TV shows, *Joe 90*, every time I looked at it. It was approximately 15ft wide, with a creamy and ceramic look. There was a big toilet sign above it and it had a distinctive front which I assumed was the door. No matter how hard I tried, I could not imagine what the inside looked like. If I had been granted three wishes, I would have used the first one to find out what inside this thing.

The day my wish was finally granted I nearly suffered a serious injury. Morufat, Karimot and I were on our way back home after going to buy doughnuts at Cullen's grocery shop. We had crossed two lanes of traffic and were waiting for the red man to turn green so that we could finish crossing the road. I was staring at the toilet as usual when it suddenly the silver doors started to open sideways and disappear into the side of the structure. An *oyinbo* man stepped out. Inside, it was brightly lit, with a porcelain toilet and sink, and a white rectangular hand dryer on the wall beside the sink. I was surprised at the actual size because it only took up half the space I had expected based on the outside. Another thing that surprised me was that I was a little disappointed that it was a normal toilet. After two weeks of obsession, it was just a normal toilet. Almost immediately, a host of new questions filled my mind: 'how was it cleaned?' and 'what if the door opened while you are using it?' As quickly as the door had opened, it suddenly closed. This seemed to jolt me out of the trance I fallen into. I ran to catch up with my sisters, while crossing the road I came inches away from being knocked down by a motorcycle.

The Telephone

... I had a fascination about the telephone from a very young age. For the six years we lived in Akobo, the neighbourhood was always supposed to be getting a telephone pole. Up until the time we left, it had still not been installed. The few places I ever saw a telephone was at the secretary's office at school, my mum's office at the hospital, my grandpa's house and at our family friend Okanala's house in Bodija. The phones were rotary-style and I was always fascinated by how it worked. I did not find out until I was fourteen. At Landward Court, there was a telephone in the sitting room and another in my parent's bedroom. When we first got the telephones, my dad showed us how to use it. I was a little disappointed because it was not a rotary telephone but I was still impressed by the design. One of the most important lessons he taught us that day was that if the phone rang, we should let it ring twice before picking up or it will cut off mid-conversation.

We had been living in Landward Court for about a month. I was home by myself one day looking out of the window when I saw a group of *oyinbo* boys pushing and shoving a younger boy. I was concerned that the boy was in trouble. After a few minutes I got the courage to call the police. I picked up the phone and dialled 999.

The operator said, 'what emergency service do you require?'

I said, 'The police'.

My heart was racing when the police operator answered, 'What is your emergency?', she asked.

'There are some boys bullying another boy outside my house', I said.

'Pardon me, I can't hear you,' she said, 'can you speak slowly please.'

I started to lose my nerve but I repeated the statement and she still could not hear me. I lost my nerve and dropped the phone. I was disappointed in myself. I looked outside my window and saw that the boy was still being harassed.

Twenty minutes after dropping the phone, the doorbell rang. I opened the door and I was shocked to see two policemen standing outside the door. My first thoughts were that my dad was going to beat me.

One of them said, 'Hello, there was an emergency call made from this house. Is everything OK?'

I started to babble like a brook and tried to explain the reason I dialled 999.

'I saw some boys bullying another boy downstairs but they have gone now.'

One of them looked at me quizzically and said, 'Are your parents at home?'

If it wasn't biologically impossible, I would have shitted a brick. I thought I was going to get my parents into trouble for leaving me home alone.

'No, they have gone to work.'

'How old are you?'

'I am 13.'

'Are you sure everything is OK.'

'Yes I am sure, thank you.'

'OK take care now.'

'Bye bye.'

I breathed a huge sigh of relief when I shut the door. I actually believed my stay in London would have been cut cruelly short if my dad had been home when this happened.

Hyde Park with Mum

… I spent some of my happiest moments in Hyde Park. It was a twenty- minute walk from Landward Court and I didn't truly appreciate it until we moved away. It was the sheer size and space which captivated me the most. There was grass as far as I could see in all directions and a lake. I would watch jealously as people rode their bikes and skated on rollerblades. Prior to this, the biggest piece of land I had ever been on was my dad's farm where he grew tomatoes and spinach, but the farm was a vegetable patch compared to the park. On one of our many trips to the park I fondly remember my mum saying, '*Kani ile ni, won ma ti so ibi bayi di oko*" (if this was home, they would have turned it into farmland). I had never been in such vast clear area which wasn't being used for farmland. There seemed to be thousands of people in the park, but because of the size it accommodated everybody comfortably. People played football, had barbecues, walked their dogs and basically enjoyed life. Going to the park in the summertime made me feel closer to home, it was relaxing and the sun often shone brightly.

I don't recall how long we were in London before we visited but my most memorable visit was on a sunny summer day in 1992. One Sunday morning, my mum asked if anyone would like to go for a walk with her and I eagerly volunteered. I asked her if we could walk to Hyde Park to buy ice cream which she agreed to. While waiting at the traffic lights to cross over the road to reach the park, I noticed a large crowd of people at the park entrance. As we got closer, it became clear that the large group were of made of between ten and fifteen smaller groups. Each group faced one direction looking at somebody who was standing on a platform talking. This was another first for me. In Nigeria, I was used to seeing crowds at the scene of car accidents where every-one would claim they saw everything that happened but would somehow give different accounts of the same event.

I asked mum what was going in and she said, 'This is called Speaker's Corner'. There was an excitement in her voice which made me anxious that she would forget or delay the primary objective of this visit which was to buy me ice cream. Some speakers had signs stating the subject they were talking about. As they spoke, a group gathered around them and often their audience would cheer or clap. I also saw an argument between a speaker and members of the crowd. It was both exciting and fascinating.

I saw an ice cream van, took my mum's hand and walked towards it. After buying my ice cream, we walked back towards Speaker's Corner. We walked around for ten minutes listening to different speakers before settling by one of the smaller groups. As we arrived, a young *oyinbo* man who was in the crowd jumped on the stage and stared speaking. He spoke for about ten minutes, and whatever he talked about made my mother laugh and the crowd applauded when he finished. The crowd thinned out while the next speaker made his preparation. I expected us to leave as well but mum used the opportunity to move closer to the stage. The next speaker was a black man with dreadlocks. From the sign he had erected behind him, I knew he was going to be speaking about Jesus. He started his talk with a lot of energy, pointing to random members of the crowds, asking questions and then answering them himself almost immediately. My mum was listening intently. He held a Bible in his hand and he was waving it vigorously in the air. He said the true word of God was in the Bible, and all other religions were fakes. I saw somebody give him a Quran.

He held it out in front of him, flicked the pages and said, 'my friends, you see all this in here, it is all gibberish and nonsense'.

I began to get angry, but before I could process my feelings I heard somebody shout, 'can you read or understand what is in there?'

I looked left to see who the defender of my faith was and saw that it was my mother. She was pointing at him and shouting, 'can you read what is in there?'

He replied, 'I don't have to be able to read it to know it is gibberish'.

'If you can't read it, how can you say it gibberish?'

At this, the crowd started to clap and murmur in agreement with my mother.

I saw the looming defeat register on the speaker's face as he waved my mum away nonchalantly. He tried to continue speaking to the crowd but he was drowned out by the same statement, this time by other voices in the crowd: 'can you read what is in there?'

The crowd started to disperse and as we left, mum called him an idiot to his face. I had always looked up to my mum, but my love and respect for her reached a higher plateau that sunny Sunday afternoon.

Pack Your Bags

... One day I was watching television when I suddenly heard a hissing noise coming from the bathroom. When I got to the bathroom, there was water all over the place. It looked like it had just rained because the floor and the walls were wet. Moruf was standing there with a shocked look on his face and holding a towel around his waist. Morufat arrived just after me and asked what happened. Moruf said, 'I don't t know' in a very unconvincing manner.

'*Ki lo nsele.*' My dad had been woken up by the commotion and he gestured for me to move out of the way so that he could enter the bathroom to see what was going on. I moved out of his way but still stood by the door and was able to hear my dad ask Moruf what happened again.

'I don't know,' he replied again.

'You pulled that thing in the middle didn't you?'

'No, I didn't.'

Dad raised his voice angrily, 'don't lie, you pulled that thing in the middle and turned on the shower. How else did this place get wet?'

It now made sense to me. Moruf had pulled the knob between the bath taps which activated the shower. I could only imagine that he had not expected the water to gush out of the shower head with such force and was not able to control it. It didn't need Hercule Poirot to work out what had happened, but Moruf continued to deny that he had pulled the knob. This infuriated my dad further and Moruf was just compounding his guilt further by continuing to lie. My dad hit him a couple of time on his back. He tried to block his blows with one hand because the other was busy holding up the towel.

As he left the bathroom, my dad looked even angrier than he had sounded.

'Clean this place up, then I will deal with you. I know you pulled it and yet you are still lying.'

He stomped off into the sitting room and I watched Moruf on his knees using a rag to clean the wet floor. After he had finished cleaning the bathroom floor, he came into the bedroom where I had come to take refuge from my dad's mood. As he was about to lie down on his bed, my dad opened the bedroom door, looked sternly at Moruf.

'O ya O ya, pack your bags, I am sending you back to Nigeria,' he said.

These words scared me to death.

'You are lying, do you think I brought you to England to become a liar? You are catching the first flight back to Muritala Airport in the morning.'

I nearly started to cry as I lay on my bed and began to imagine what would happen if Moruf got sent back.

He would probably have to and live with my grandmother Olomowewe. This thought filled me with dread. From what I remembered, it was not a place

I wanted my brother growing up in. While I was letting my imagination run wild, Moruf had started to put some of his clothes in a blue suitcase. When dad left the room, I saw Moruf smirk. I could not believe what I seeing, I was laying there worried half to death and this fool was smiling. Didn't he understand the gravity of the situation he had put himself? He had barely been in England for two months, now he was getting sent back to Nigeria. If I had taken the time to think about things practically like Moruf, I should have known that that dad was only making empty threats. I guess Moruf already knew this because the likelihood of dad spending money on a plane ticket and booking a flight within twelve hours because of a misdemeanour was pretty slim.

An hour later, dad came into the bedroom to check that Moruf had backed his bag. The next morning, dad did not follow up on his threat. In fact, I don't remember Moruf being punished for the shower incident. For the next couple of months, dad issued the same threat whenever any of us did anything wrong: 'pack your bags, you are going back to Nigeria'. He stopped making the threats after a while because he saw that it was not having the desired effect.

The Barbershop

... My dad decided to take Moruf and I to a barber shop that he used to visit regularly when he lived in London in the Seventies. On the way there, he regaled us with stories about how Brixton was the place to be in the Seventies. From what he told us during the journey, I was expecting Brixton and the barber shop to be a high class area. When we got off the tube, I was in for another disappointment.

My first impressions of Brixton can best be described as bizarre. It was noisy, not very clean and I had not seen such a large congregation of black people in one place since we left Muritala Muhammad Airport. We walked through a market which was tiny and very neat compared to some the markets back home. We then walked through some alleyways which I wouldn't have entered in the dark and finally arrived at the famous barbershop.

It was very small but six barber chairs were crammed in there. We all sat down on three empty chairs and waited. While waiting, I noticed that at least six different people came into the shop, went into a backroom with one of the barbers and left again. I thought this was quite odd and I kept looking in that direction. All of the sudden I caught my dad's eye. He was giving me one of those stern looks which didn't need words to make the message clear: 'face front and mind your own business'. After about twenty minutes of waiting, the barber who kept going into the back room became available. He looked at me and said 'next'. I really didn't want him to cut my hair so I looked at my dad with a look to say 'please don't let him cut my hair'. I guess my look was not as clear as the one he had given me earlier because he motioned for me to go and sit in the chair.

I sat in the chair and the barber spoke in a strong Jamaican accent.

'What ya want bredrin?'

This was the first time I had heard this accent and I could not understand what he was saying at all. I just looked at him blankly.

'Blad how you want me cut your hair?' he asked again.

'Pardon,' I said.

I could not believe he was speaking in English, this was the first time I had heard the Jamaican accent in my whole life.

My dad saw that I was in some difficulty and he came to my rescue and told the man to just cut it low. While this man was cutting my hair, he left me three times and went into the backroom with people who came into the shop. On one of these occasions, I saw him and another man exchange something discreetly which I could not see. I felt very uneasy and saw a worried and disappointed look on dad's face. I guess Brixton had changed a lot from the time he had last visited. It wasn't until some years later which I was able to make hypothesis why the barber kept going into the back room.

Omolewa Nursery and Primary School

… My last report card at my previous school in Nigeria, the Omolewa Nursery and Primary School, showed that out of a class of thirty, I was ranked number twenty-five in terms of intelligence. I found the schoolwork very difficult, especially mathematics and always tried to look inconspicuous when a teacher asked a question. But trying to look inconspicuous made me stand out more. I tried another tactic of raising my hand along with the other students but sometimes the teacher would still pick me to answer the question. I often got beaten if I didn't know the answer to the questions.

I wasn't the most popular kid in the school either. I was not the fastest, I was not very good at football and I was not one of the strongest. As soon as my mum or dad dropped me at 8am, I was praying for the end of the day to come. Worst of all, I hated the beating and the punishments. Some of the punishments dished out by those bastard teachers included beating me on the back of my hand with the edge of the ruler, making me stand with one leg in the air or stand facing the wall with my hands in air. The worst of the punishment was called 'stool down': this involved standing on one leg and bending over with one finger on the floor for balance. If two fingers or the second leg touched the floor, the beating received would be unbearable. Two of the most common tools used to beat the kids were a *koboko* which is three ropes made of cow hide tied together. The other tool is called a *pankere* which is a long cane made of bamboo. For added effect, some of the teachers would soak the cane in water before beating the kids with it.

My greatest ambition during my time Omolewa was to be part of the school drum band. One of the prerequisites for joining the band was that the boys had to be in Primary 6. I was not eligible to join because I would only be in Primary 6 for only two months before I left the school. I have always wondered what life would have been like if I had been able to join the drum band before coming to England. In addition to playing the national anthem every morning during school assembly, they always went to represent the schools during sporting competitions.

Every morning I would stare at them enviously during assembly waiting for my turn. I think that the only time I felt sad after it was confirmed that we were coming to England was when I realised that I wouldn't be fulfilling my dream about joining the drum band. As part of the morning routines at Omolewa, students were allocated shifts to sweep the whole class and clean the blackboards every morning before classes started. At 8am, the school prefect rang the bell to inform everyone to get gather for assembly. All students would line up according to their classes and then according to height.

Assembly always started with the recitation of the National Anthem. We were all required to put our right arms across our chests with our palm resting on our left shoulder. Then we had to recite the anthem in unison. Knowing the national anthem word for word was a mandatory requirement at school. If it wasn't biologically impossible I would say all school kids were born with the ability to recite the anthem while in the womb.

After the national anthem we would sing hymns. I didn't always sing along, firstly because I was a Muslim but most of time it was because my hymn book was usually in tatters. At random points, the school owners would come to assembly to give a speech and inspect the students. The students called the founder of the school 'Mummy School' and her daughter, who actually ran the school, we called 'Aunty Ronke'. I didn't really like the daughter, I found her very rude and pretentious. She always had an aura of snobbery about her. She acted like she was better than everybody in the school which is a trait I have always disliked from a very young age.

The students' appearance was something that they always examined whenever they came to assembly. Depending on their mood, they could decide that all the kids that were the neatest and tidiest should make their way to the front of the assembly to be praised. Or they could decide that those who looked dirty and untidy should be shamed in front of the whole school. The teachers would walk along the rows of students to see who met the requirements of the day and sent them to the front. For the first five years I was in the school, I was never picked to go for being the tidiest or dirty, I was just average.

Kabir Omolewa - Back row, 6th from the right to left

Three incidents really defined my time at Omolewa. One day when I was in Primary 5, I went to school looking immaculate. I had washed my white knee length socks with extra OMO washing powder the day before and spent extra time ironing my school uniform the night before. I went to these extra lengths because my class teacher had told us that Mummy School was coming to assembly the next day. I really wanted to get picked to go to the front of the school and get praised.

The next morning, the time came for the teachers to pick the best-looking students to represent their class in front of the school. My class teacher started to inspect the kids in her class. She picked a couple of students before she reached me. She looked at me from top to bottom. My heart was beating so fast because I knew she was going to pick me.

'OK you, go to the front.'

I swelled with pride. I was one of the chosen. I stepped out of the line with a massive smile on my face and started to walk towards the front. Finally I was going to be praised and adulated by the whole school. I had all these pictures in my head: I would tell my dad what happened when he came to pick us up after school. He would say, 'that's my boy', and buy me meat pie on the way home. I would write a letter to my mum who was in London and she would be so proud of me also. I had taken approximately five or six steps to praise and adulation when I heard, 'stop, come back, you have something on your trousers'. My teacher noticed a brown mark on my green shorts. My dream had been had become a reality and turned into a nightmare within five seconds. I nearly started crying on the spot but I kept my composure and I retook my place in line. I did not join when it was time to start clapping for the kids who had made the cut. I just kept thinking I should amongst them. Upon inspection when I got home later that day, I concluded that the mark was made by the iron.

'SHAME, SHAME, SHAME,' the children chanted.

I finally made it to the front of the whole school during morning assembly a few weeks later but it wasn't for the reason I had hoped for. On the morning I stood in front of the 300 students, I hadn't washed my socks for the previous three days when I got home from school as usual, and I paid a painful price. I knew it was risky but I was being very lazy so I decided to take it. I tried to hide behind the kids in front of me and prayed that this humiliation would end quickly.

On that fateful morning, my socks were not as white as they should have been. In fact, they were closer to brown than white. I wanted to avoid my dad seeing my socks so I quickly entered the car and waited with the driver. During the drive to school, I felt very uneasy because I had a bad feeling that I was going to regret not washing my socks. During assembly, I prayed that there would not be a surprise visit by Mummy School or Aunty. I recited 'Al Fatia' from the Quran over and over, hoping for a miracle.

My heart nearly jumped out of my chest when I saw Aunty coming down the stairs to my right. When she started her speech I knew that my fate was sealed. It was about the importance of looking neat and tidy when representing Omolewa. She said that all the children who looked dirty were not the kind the students wanted at this school. She instructed the teachers to send all the dirty kids in their classes to the front so that they can be shamed in front of the whole school. My class teacher walked amongst the students and told the usual suspects to go to the front. The closer she got to me the faster my heart beat. Maybe she won't see me or she had reached her quota. Sadly, I was deserted by prayers and miracles in my time of need. She looked at me from top to bottom. The moment I saw her looking at my socks I knew I was doomed. She said, 'umph', tapped me on my shoulder and motioned for me to make my way to front. I took a deep breath, got out of line and took the walk of shame past my classmates. As soon I went past the first person in the line I felt like I had fallen into a bottomless black hole. Walking towards the spot where the dirty chosen were standing, it felt like all eyes were on me. I quickly made my way behind the seven or eight people already there and prayed that none of my family friends saw me. While cowering and waiting for this humiliation to end. I looked at the people around me and I felt a great injustice had been inflicted on me. These people's clothes were dirty, their shoes were battered and ripped, and they looked extremely poor. How dare they group me amongst 'these people'? I lived in a three bedroom house, came to school in a chauffeur-driven car and my mum was currently in London. Before that she had been in Saudi Arabia, their parent had probably never been to the airport. (I did not realise how snobbish I was being till years later. I have always cringed whenever I have remembered my thoughts at that time and I now believe this was my most shameful moment of that morning. I guess I was not very different from Aunty Ronke!).

I missed the major part of what Ronke had said, but caught the last part: 'we don't want these dirty children in this school, shame on them'. At once and in harmony, the whole assembly started chanting, 'SHAME, SHAME', with their palms facing outwards towards us for emphasis. I wanted the ground to open up and swallow me up. At that moment in time I realised how much I missed my mum. I really wanted her to come and shield me from this humiliation but she was thousands of miles away in London. When I got home that day, I washed all my socks, went into my bedroom and cried. I had gone through one of the most humiliating moments in my young life. Although it had been my fault, I knew that if my mum was around she would comfort me. I missed her so much when she was away, my dad did his best to compensate but there's nothing like a mother's touch.

The third incident happened in early December 1991 and involved a boy called Bayo. One day, I saw him bullying my best friend David during break time and I intervened to protect my friend. We had a verbal altercation and he told me to mind my own business because the situation didn't concern me. He threatened to beat up but I just laughed at him because he was so short, I knew I could beat him up easily.

Later on that day after school, as I made my way to get some water from the school kitchen, I was suddenly surrounded by Bayo and three of his friends under the oak tree where most of the kids hung out. I had seen them too late so there was nowhere to run. As they closed in on me from fours corners, I prepared for the inevitable beating I was about to receive. I made fists, bent my knees and started to spin and kick all around me. I planned to punch at least one of them hard and my target was Bayo. All of a sudden I heard 'get him', all four of them came at me at once and began reigning blows on me. Before I could process the pain from the blows to the face, I felt punches in my stomach, before I could process that pain; I felt hits on my legs and thighs as I was kicked on my left and right side simultaneously. I tried hard to punch Bayo, but my efforts were futile. As quickly as it started, it was over. As I watched Bayo and his gang walk away feeling victorious, I vowed revenge on all four of them and took solace in the fact that I had stayed on my feet. This was the main reason I did not cry.

I began to plan my revenge in the car as my mum drove home that afternoon. Moruf was at secondary school at that point so I could not call on him to assist me. I had some level of protection when Morufat and Moruf attended Omolewa with me but as soon as they left, I was fair game. I calculated that I had two weeks to execute my plan for revenge. School was due to break up for the Christmas holidays and I would not be returning for the new term in January 1992 because we would soon be departing for London. During the next week, I could not get any of them alone because they either moved everywhere in their foursome or in doubles.

On the morning of my last Monday at Omolewa, I saw one of boys who rushed me standing alone buying *puff puff (doughnut)*. I snuck up behind and punched him hard in the back of his head. He screamed, fell face down and all *his puff puff* fell on the ground. He turned around while lying on the floor and held the back of his head. I saw the fear in his eyes when he realised who I was and I suddenly felt sorry for him. I thought he was going to get up and fight but he stayed on the ground, I turned around and walked away feeling victorious. One down, three to go.

On the Wednesday, I was coming out of the toilets when I saw the second member of Bayo's crew coming into the toilet. Without thinking, I head butted him right in his face, he fell to the ground, screwed up his face and began to cry. I did not feel sorry for him because he was Bayo's main lieutenant. Some of the other kids who saw what happened stared at me with a looks of sheer bewilderment. Later on that afternoon I was standing by the swings when I saw the third member of Bayo's crew approaching me. I quickly scanned around me just in case they were going to jump me again, I was relieved when I didn't see anybody else. I thought he was coming to fight me so I approached him, prepared to do battle. As we got closer he suddenly said,

'Kabiru, ma bi nu'.

I was shocked and in two minds. I wanted to beat him up badly but I could not bring myself to do it after he had just apologised. He must have heard about how I dealt with his friends and he wanted to avoid the same fate. He said sorry again and I could see the relief in his eyes when I said '*ma worry*'. (don't worry)

On the Wednesday night I decided my revenge on Bayo would sweeter if I beat him up on the last day of the school term which would be on Friday. I felt it would be good way to sign off and leave a lasting legacy of my time at Omolewa. I saw him a couple of times by himself on Thursday and it took a lot self restraint for me not to dive on him and start punching him in his face. I was seething with anger every time I saw him, I truly hated his face and wanted to do him serious injury. I wanted to humiliate the little shrimp but my desire to leave a legacy superseded my anger and I decided to wait till Friday. There would be no consequence because I was going to

London and would not be returning to the school for the new term. I could not wait to get to school on the Friday morning. I was care-free and felt infallible, all I could think about was' I am going to beat up Bayo and then I am going to London'. I planned to beat him up during the break regardless of who he was with. I didn't care if I got rushed again as long I landed at least one solid blow in his smug face.

During assembly, I was a little disconcerted when I didn't see Bayo at his usual spot at the front of line (he was the shortest in our class so he was always at the front). I hoped that he was just running late. I was despondent by 11am when I realised that Bayo would not be coming to school that day. I asked his twin brother Dayo where his brother was and he confirmed that he not coming to school because he was sick. I felt so angry and cheated, not beating up Bayo when I had the opportunity on the Thursday will always be one the biggest regrets of my life. (20 years on, I am still seething that I did not beat up that little shrimp when I had the chance, I am still looking for him).

As my mum drove me out of the gates of Omolewa for the last time that afternoon, I was ecstatic that I would not be returning to the school, but also wished that I could come back just once more before we left for London so that I could take my revenge.

Christ Church Bentick Primary School

... One of the stories my dad told me before leaving Nigeria was that going to school in England was mandatory. He said that parents could get sent to prison if their kids didn't go to school and there was a special squad which went round looking for kids who didn't go to school. Best of all, there was no beating allowed in schools. This was like music to my ears.

Two weeks after moving into Landward Court, I was itching to leave the house and go to school. I was bored out of my brains staying at home while waiting for my parents to find a school for Karimot and I. We hadn't bought a television yet at that point, so we did our best to entertain each other playing games from back home. My mum tried to get Karimot and I into a primary which was literally a minute from our building. We were rejected due to lack of space. My mum told me a few years later that she believed that the real reason was because we were African.

She finally got us into a school which was about ten minutes away from our flat. I couldn't believe how excited I was when my mum told us that she had got us into a primary school. It wasn't because I liked school, I just wanted get out of the house. On the morning of what would be my first day, I was excited and terrified at the same time. I imagined that I would be the only black kid in class and would be the focus of all the attention. We ate our breakfast and got dressed to go. My mum had bought us each a coat and some new clothes especially for school. I had been surprised when she told me that we would not be wearing a school uniform. We walked for approximately fifteen minutes and I was unimpressed I was when we first saw the school. It was a long two-storey building with a concrete playground outside. Inside, it had lots of paintings on the walls. The name of the school was Christ Church Bentick Primary School and it looked very different to Omolewa.

Walking into the reception, Karimot and I sat down while my mum spoke to the receptionist. We waited for approximately ten minutes before Karimot's teacher came to came to collect her. Five minutes later my teacher came to collect me. She was a tall ginger-haired woman who wore glasses. She shook my hand firmly and gently said hello. I was so nervous I mumbled something that sounded like hello but I can't say for sure. She spoke to my mum for a couple of minutes before she motioned for me to follow her. My mum hugged me and said she would come and pick us outside after school.

I followed my new teacher as she took me to my new class. We walked up some stairs and with every stair I took, I felt like turning back and running after my mother, to beg her to take me back home with her. I finally made it to my class and it was too late to turn back. We walked in and thirty faces turned to look at me. I had never seen so many different races in one place in my life. It was like a United Nations Assembly. There were whites, blacks and Asians kids too, which was a bit of a shock because I was expecting to see just *oyinbo* kids. With my legs shaking and my heart pounding, I took off my coat and put it on the hook. Miss T asked me to stand in front of the class and say something about myself.

I walked slowly to the centre of the class.

'Good morning, my name is Kabir Kareem, I come from Nigeria. I came here with my parents, two sisters and one brother on the 12th January. I like reading and running.'

I felt I said it in such an articulate and concise manner that they were bound to be impressed with my English. I quickly surveyed my new classroom which looked very very different from my old one. My old class had the bare minimum in it: thirty chairs and tables, the teacher's desk and a long blackboard. My new class here was lively and colourful. There were six tables each with six chairs around it. There were hand drawn pictures and paintings by the students over the walls, a games section and two computers.

All tables were assigned names and the teacher told me to go to table Bumble. When I sat down there were five smiling faces looking at me and only one of them was *oyinbo*. There were two black boys named Dan and Andrew, one black girl, one *oyinbo* girl who looked as pale as a ghost, and one Asian boy. They all introduced themselves and I was very shocked at the accents of the *dudu* (black) boys. I think I subconsciously expected to hear American accents. I inadvertently embarrassed the black girl because of my reaction to something I had never ever seen before in my life. When she introduced herself, she smiled and I shocked to see her mouth filled with metal instead of teeth. My shock must have been evident in my face because the smile quickly disappeared and she put her hand over her hand. I felt awful but I could not understand why she would have metal in her mouth instead of teeth, it reminded me of Jaws from the James Bond movies. Dan told me that the table I was sitting on was the games table. I could not believe what this boy was telling me. He confirmed that I was currently sitting on a table where we supposed to play games. I still could not believe my ears, there was an assigned table to play games, although they were 'educational' games. There were other tables for art, reading and other activities which I can't remember.

I was very apprehensive about being the dumbest kid in class and thought I would be way behind everybody else. The first lesson on my first day was Geography. The teacher asked, 'What is the capital of the USA?' I was expecting all hand to go up, eager to answer this easy question. I looked around and not one single person put their hand up. I just thought that maybe they were shy because there was a new kid in class. After a minute, the teacher said, 'The capital of USA is Washington DC'. She then asked for the capital of France. I looked around and again nobody put their hand up. I decided to be bold and put my hand up. 'Yes Kabia?' She pronounced name wrongly but I didn't think much of it at the time. As I stood up I noticed everybody looking at me strangely.

I said, 'the capital of France is Paris'. I sat back down.

'Very good Kabia, well done.'

A girl on another table put her hand up to answer the next questions and I was gobsmacked when she didn't stand up. I stared at her until she saw me looking and

I quickly looked away. The next few students who answered questions didn't stand up either. The bizarre looks I received a few minutes previously suddenly made sense. They must have found it strange when I stood up and I found it strange when they stayed sat down to answer the questions.

Dan and an *oyinbo* boy named Thomas were assigned to be my buddies. They were supposed to show me round and help me to settle in. During the first break, I asked Thomas to show me where the toilet was. When he spoke, I was surprised that he didn't sound at all like the *oyinbo* people on TV. He took me down the stairs next to the reception. As we walked in to the toilet, I couldn't help but remember the toilet at Omolewa, which was literally a shit-hole. It stank, the plumbing didn't work and I only used when I was left with no other choice. This toilet was clean, well lit and most importantly the plumbing worked. Again, I will never forget what happened next for as long as I live. Thomas began to give me a tutorial on how to use the lavatory. He pointed to the urinals and said this is what you use when you want to pee. I had never heard urinating described as 'pee' before but I understood what he was trying to say. He then took me into the cubical pointed at the porcelain toilet and said 'this is used to poo'. He then proceeded to demonstrate, fully clothed how to use the toilet and then showed me how to flush it. I felt like slapping him across his face but I just smiled and nodded. On hindsight, I guess he was trying to help me because he assumed that because I was from Africa, I didn't know how to use the toilet.

After the toilet incident, I went outside for what I later found out it was the first of three break-times. I saw the kids playing with hula hoops, footballs, tennis balls and basketballs. I thought I had died and gone to heaven. At Omolewa, my friends and I played football on gravel and there were daily fights for the only fun thing in the school: the swings. Sometimes there were at least sixteen people waiting their turn to go on the swings. If you didn't know the person who was the first to claim the swing on that day, you were not getting a turn.

I went to look for Karimot and I found her playing with some new friends. She was already settling in. I sat on one of the benches and looked at the kids playing games painted on the concrete floors and walls. As I watched them playing hopscotch, I couldn't help but break into a smile at the major difference between Nigeria and England over a simple game of hopscotch. In London the game could only be played in a designated area. In Nigeria, it was played anywhere there was sand; all that was needed was a stick to draw the boxes and the game would begin. I had never felt so lonely in my life, I suddenly began to miss my friends at Omolewa and Akobo. All of a sudden there was a loud whistle and the most surreal thing I had ever seen happened. Every single kid in the play ground stood still. Approximately five seconds later, a whistle was blown for the second time, everybody ran in different directions and formed separate lines. I sat where I was and just watched in amazement. I didn't know which line my class was in and so I joined the back of the first line I could. One by one, each line started to walk to their respective classrooms. I followed the line I had joined until I could slip away and make my way back to my classroom.

The return to class was uneventful until lunchtime when Thomas took me into the dining hall which was filled with hundreds of kids. There was no table with two spaces available so he and I had to sit on separate tables. When I sat down, nobody seemed to care that I was there because they were all looking at a particular teacher. I would shortly find out why nobody gave a damn that I was there. There was queue at the other side of the hall. At the head of this queue were big shiny silver contraptions with four *oyinbo* women wearing aprons standing behind them. I did not know the procedure for getting lunches so I sat there tried to look as inconspicuous as possible.

All of a sudden, there was a massive commotion and in one swift motion, all the kids on my table made a mad dash for the queue on the other side of the hall. I was too shocked to move. I was the only one left on the table and only stood up when one of the dinner ladies beckoned for me to go and join queue. While waiting in the queue, I was nervous about doing something else wrong so I copied the kids in front of me. I picked up a tray, a plate and cutlery. When I reached the front, I was met with an assortment of foods, sausages, fish fingers, carrots, rice and something white which looked like *fufu* (I later found out it was mashed potato). This was world's apart from lunch at Omolewa where you were served a big spoon of food in the classroom. One major rule was that if you didn't bring your plate, you didn't eat. Here, I was so shocked by the variety of food on offer that I began to salivate.

I stood rooted to the spot for a few seconds then I heard one of the dinner ladies say, 'what do you want love?' I gave her my plate and I just started to point at the things I wanted. She put some on a plate and I moved along until I got to the dessert section. I had picked up a bowl earlier but I didn't know what it was for. I later found out bowls are picked at the front if you only wanted custard. When I got to the desert section, there was a row of bowls with chocolate cake in it. I saw the kids in front of me picking up a bowl and then one of the dinners ladies pouring something yellow on top of it. When I got to my turn, the lady asked for my bowl and poured the yellow stuff on it. I could not understand why I didn't get cake but I was new so I just took my food and left.

It took me a few minutes to find my seat, everything looked the same. I put my tray on the table and sat down. Before I began to eat the food, I looked around me quickly and was shocked by what I saw. These *oyinbo* kids did not know how to hold a knife and fork; most of them held the fork in the right hand and the knife on the left. When I was taught how to hold cutlery, it was based on how the English did it, so I could not understand why these English kids were holding it the wrong way round.

I was so eager to taste the yellow food that I woofed down my main course. I really enjoyed the fish fingers and mashed potatoes, but the carrots were a bit soft. The yellow stuff looked like *ogi/pap* (blended corn in custard form) which was one of my favourite foods. Unfortunately, it tasted nothing like ogi/*pap*. My first taste of what I later found out was custard was not pleasant and because of that I did not eat custard for at least another four years. It felt like I had just been force-fed vomit. Swallowing the custard forced the fish fingers and carrots I had just eaten moments earlier to make reappearance on my plate. I vomited most of my lunch. Everybody on the table looked at me and I saw a couple of kids sniggering. I did not really care, there was no way I was going to eat the rest of the custard in the bowl.

After lunch, I went outside not knowing what to expect because I was new and everything so far had been very different from what I was used to. There were kids playing and running around. I started to scan around looking for a familiar face from the table in my class. I could not find anyone so I went to down to a bench and watched everybody playing. I saw Karimot coming out of the building. She was walking and laughing with some kids in her class. She looked like she had been coming to the school for years. She saw me, waved and continued to play with her friends. I felt alone and exposed sitting on the bench, so I decided to go back to the classroom.

When I reached my classroom door, I felt a sense of adventure so I carried on walking. A few yards from my class I reached a small lounge which stopped me dead in my tracks. On the right hand side was a bookshelf which reached the ceiling and it was full of books. The sight of all these books, glorious books, took my breath away. The only experience I can now equate to how I felt as I stared at the books back then is orgasmic. I was delirious with joy, my knees began to shake, and I started to salivate again. I wanted to touch them but I stood rooted to the spot and tried to make sense of where I was. I felt like Ali Baba when he discovered the treasure cave. I composed myself and took a book off the shelf. It was called *Treasure Island*. I had read the beginning and the end of the book a few months earlier but the copy I read did not have a front cover and whole sections in the middle was missing. I was holding in my hand a hardcover copy which was a lot thicker than my old copy. I picked another book from another part of the shelf. It was *Gulliver's Travels*, I picked another one, *Jack and the Beanstalk*, and another, *Little Red Riding Hood*. This was beyond my wildest dreams.

'Hello Kabia'. It was Miss T.

'Good afternoon, Miss. Can I read these books?'

'Of course you can, you can use this library anytime you want. You can even take them home as long you bring them back.'

It took a lot of self-restraint for me not to jump on her and kiss her. I was so happy I wanted to cry. I was in my own personal utopia. My most precious memories of my time at Christ Church were the many hours I spent in the Library.

The elation I felt when I saw the library at Christ Church was multiplied tenfold when I walked into the Marylebone library the weekend after I started school. It was ten times the size of my school library and I became giddy at sight of the thousands of books. For me, it was the equivalent of the entering the libraries in Timbuktu or the Ancient Library of Alexandria.

The Television

... I came home one day from school by myself. It was two weeks or three weeks after I started school and Karimot was at the after school club. When I opened the door, my mum was standing by the kitchen door with a disappointed look on her face. I remember thinking, 'why would she be so disappointed to see, what have I done?'

I greeted her and a smile appeared on her face.

'I was hoping it would have arrived before you got home, I wanted to surprise you.'

'Surprise me with what?'

'Don't worry, you will soon find out.'

With this she went back into the kitchen and I went into my bedroom to change out of my school clothes.

Twenty minutes after I arrived, the doorbell rang and I saw my mum almost skipping to go and open the door. I watched inquisitively as she opened the door, I saw an *oyinbo* man holding a clipboard and at his feet was a large brown box. My mum signed the clipboard, handed it back to the man, and bent down to pick up the box. As she turned around, I could not contain my excitement as deciphered the picture on the box. It was a television.

I wanted to jump on my mum to give her a big kiss, but I wasn't able to because she was holding the TV. In that moment, the look of disappointment she had earlier made sense: she wanted the TV to be set up before we arrived home from school but the delivery company had been late. I was also a little disappointed that it didn't work out like that either because it would have been one the best surprises in my entire life.

My love for television was immense from when I could walk and talk. Any time my dad felt that we were watching too much television, he would say to us in a pleading tone: 'Please go and read your books. Mark my words, they will repeat what you are watching now over and over again. You will get sick of it'. It would only be years later that those words would ring true to me.

One of the main reasons why getting the television that day was so significant was because it reminded me of one of the most profound moments in my short life. After Morufat had tuned the TV that evening, I was watching the seven o'clock news with my mum and I suddenly remembered something that had happened a few years previously in Nigeria.

I was about nine years old and was watching TV with my mother one evening when she changed the channel to one which was showing my favourite Yoruba parable songs. I began to sing along as I usually did. I suddenly saw my mum watching me intently with a smile on her face. She had never heard me sing the song before because she had been abroad; I wanted to impress her so I continued singing along word for word. I sang with utter joy and freedom.

Nje o bu moo
Mo bu moo

Kini nje moo?
Molade
Kini nje ade?
Adesipo
Kini nje po?
Ipo sere
Kini nje isere?
Isere omoyo
Kini nje omoyo?
Omo akoko
Kini nje akoko?
Akoko orisa
Kini nje orisa?
Orisa alaye
Kini nje alaye?
Alaye Olorun
Kini olorun?
Olorun ekolo
Kini nje ekolo?
Ekolo ajuba
Kini nje ajuba?
Ajuba iyere
Kini nje iyere?
Iyere mogun
Kini nje mogun?
Mogun onire
Kini nje onire?
Inire iye
Kini nje iye?
Iya asa
Kini nje asa?
Asa oke
Kini nje oke?

Oke ile
Kini nje ile?
Ile owu
Kini nje owu?
Owu aso
Kini nje aso?
Aso ni mo ro
Igi lo ro
Aso ni mo wo yi
Igi lo wo yen
Aso ni mo ro igi lo ro....

She smiled at me when I finished, which filled me with a tremendous amount of joy. As her smile began to fade, a look of slight despondency appeared on her face. I was initially confused but the reason for the look was soon revealed. Looking at me adoringly, she said wistfully:

'Kani bi o se mo iwe ni yen…'. (If only you knew your books this well…)

The look on her face suddenly made sense. She was very impressed and proud of my ability to memorise things I saw on TV but could not understand why I struggled in school. I guess it was a bitter-sweet moment for her because she could see potential in my abilities but was also disappointed that I did not apply them to my schoolwork. Those words weighed heavily on me over the next few weeks and I tried harder in school, but the incident soon faded into memory.

I did not think about that event again until the evening in Landward Court. I looked at my mum and smiled, this was the first of many times that events in London would take me on a nostalgic trip back to my childhood in Nigeria.

Reborn

… After my first couple of months at Christ Church, I felt like I had been reborn. I had actually come to enjoy going to school. From the perspective of an eleven year-old kid from Nigeria, primary school in England was pretty easy. Before coming to school in England, I wouldn't have described myself as academically gifted. When it came to the work we were given in my class, I sometimes felt like a genius. I wouldn't portray the work as easy, but it wasn't as challenging as some of the subjects back home. I also found that although they delivered similar subjects as my old school, but here I found them a lot easier and more enjoyable.

The subjects that I was being taught in Year 7 in Christ Church had already been taught in Primary 5 at Omolewa. On my second day, Miss T said, 'Class, we are going to have a pop quiz'. I instantly became very apprehensive. It took me a couple of minutes to remember that this was Christ Church and not Omolewa and I would not get beaten if I was not able to answer a question. By the end of quiz, I was sure there would be no doubt that I was one of the brightest pupils in the class. Miss T said the quiz was going to be a combination of

Maths, English and Geography. The whole class let a unanimous groan of protest when the teacher said there would be no calculators allowed for the Maths section. I could not understand what the fuss was about, calculators were not allowed in my old school.

The class was split into teams. My team consisted of Dan, Thomas and a couple of girls. The first question asked was: 'What is seven times seven?' I could not believe my eyes when nobody put their hands up. I put my hand up. When Miss T acknowledged me, I stood up and answered the question. She said, 'that's correct Kabia, well done'. The next question was something to do with finding the adjectives in a sentence. I was in dreamland: these were really easy questions which I knew the answers to. Every time I answered a question correctly, my team clapped and cheered. Thomas was overly excited and I got the impression that he was feeling thrilled he had been chosen to be the buddy of the brainy African. I kept getting patted on the back and getting the thumbs up. I can only describe what I was feeling at that moment in time as euphoric. I had gone from the dumb kid who sat at the back of the class to the centre of attention who wasn't afraid to put his hand up to answer a question.

During my second week we had a PE lesson. I had always enjoyed physical education back in Omolewa. Although I was only officially the fifteenth fastest boy in my class, it was a chance to get out of the classroom. The night before my first PE class at Christ Church, I was so excited I could hardly sleep. I believe there was an extra skip in my step during my walk to school on that morning. The PE lesson was going to be after the first break and I didn't concentrate on my work all morning.

After the first break, I went down to the boy's toilet with Thomas, Dan and some of the boys in my class to get changed.

The PE lesson was taken by a female teacher which I found unusual because all the PE teachers at Omolewa were men. We started the session off by doing some star jumps and stretches. I couldn't understand some of the terminology the teacher was using so I copied what everybody was doing. After ten minutes, she said that we should all line up against the fence for a race. She split the class into a boys' and a girls' group, with the girls running first. During the girl's race, I started to feel very nervous and negative thoughts started to go through my head: 'what if I come last?' and 'what if I trip and fall, they will all laugh at me and then nobody will be my friend'.

There was nothing I could do about it, then the teacher told all the boys to line up against the fence. She instructed us to run to the other end of the playground, touch the wall and run back to the fence. There were twelve boys and we all lined up against the wire fence and waited for the whistle. My heart was beating faster than a humming bird's wing. I must have heard the whistle a second late because by the time I reacted everybody else was off the line. My worst nightmare was coming true. I was going to be worse in this school than I was in the last one. I ran as fast as my legs would take me and I went past three or four people before I reached the wall. On the way back, I ran past one person, then another, then another. At the end of the race, I came second. I couldn't believe it, I came second! Everybody came around me and started to tap me on the back. I felt like a celebrity and revelled in the adulation. I had a bad feeling when I caught a boy named George giving me an evil look.

He was the one I had beaten into third place and he would go on to become one of my most bitter enemies until the end of my schooling years later. I later found that he usually came second after a boy named Anthony. He didn't come second again after I arrived.

The next day, during the first break, I was sitting on my regular bench when one of the Asian kids in my class came and asked me if I wanted to play tag. 'What is that?' I asked. He explained that that somebody will touch me and then I have to chase and try touching everybody else. There was an allocated section called home which would be safe from the tagger. This was a game that didn't need further explanation because it was universal.

I followed him to the corner of the playground where four or five of our classmates including the girl with the metal teeth were waiting. The Asian boy quickly touched me on my shoulder and said 'you are it'. Then he and the other kids ran away. We played for another fifteen minutes and I was never 'it' for the rest of the game. They all tried to catch me but I was just too agile for them. I feigned left but moved right in one swift movement with the speed of a pugilist. When one girl was inches from touching my head, I bobbed and weaved in a way that would have made Muhammad Ali proud. I still remember the baffled look on her face as she was clearly thinking, 'how could I miss?' I was so good at evading capture that a small crowd formed to watch me and they all looked stunned. I kept laughing throughout because I was enjoying myself so much, I was in my element. The Asian boy asked how I became so good at playing tag. I said, 'I don't know'.

My exploits were the talk of the class for the rest of the afternoon. Upon reflection, one of the reasons I was so good at tag was the amount time I had spent playing it in Nigeria. During the summer holidays television didn't start till 4pm if there was electricity. So between 9am and 4pm, there was nothing to do but play outside. We lived in a house with one of the biggest compounds in Akobo, so a lot of time the neighbourhood kids would come to our house to play hide and seek, tag or just climb trees for the sake of it. My one claim to fame was that I had climbed one of the tallest paw-paw trees in Akobo. All my friends had tried to do it but I was the first and only one to reach the top. Climbing trees was one of my favourite pastimes; that was one of the things I missed the most when we came to England.

Culture Shock

… The daily routine of our school days soon became set in stone. Karimot and I would wake up around 7:30am. We would have a bath separately, eat breakfast and would leave the house by 8:30am with our mum. She walked us to the school gate, say goodbye then meet at the same spot at 3:30pm for the walk home.

One day, Karimot and I met and waited at the gate at 3:30pm as usual, but mum wasn't there. I assumed she was running late so we waited a little longer. After ten minutes, I decided we should walk home. Karimot was reluctant but I convinced her that if we took the same route home we would surely run into her. We walked home without meeting her on the way. There was nobody in the flat when we got in which got me really worried. Within two minutes of entering, the front door opened and my mum walked in. I thought I would get into trouble because we did not wait for her but she had a wide smile on her face. She told us she wanted to see if we would be able to find out way home by ourselves. She had followed us every inch of the way home and said she was proud of us for being able to make our way home by ourselves. That was my first taste of independence and after that we began to make our own way to and from schools.

There were quite a few cultural shocks that I had to deal with in my first three months in London. I was very surprised at the poor spoken English of some of my new classmates. I had expected them to speak like my favourite Englishman, Roger Moore, but their grammar was awful. I felt that they were lazy speakers because they sometimes omitted to use nouns and adjectives in sentences. It took me two weeks to understand 'innit' meant 'isn't it'. There was an occasion during my first week when I asked someone for a 'biro'. The girl looked at me like I was speaking Chinese. I knew I wasn't but her response was to give me that stupid look again and said, 'Whaaat?' I pointed to what I wanted, she picked it up and said 'Oh en, you want my pen'.

Later on that same day, the same girl tapped me on the shoulder.

'Can I burrow your rubber please'.

I replied, 'Sorry I don't have a rubber band'.

The whole table burst into a spontaneous laughter. I could not understand why they found what I just said so funny. She picked up an eraser from my desk and said, 'this is called a rubber'. From that day onwards, I never referred to the pen as a biro or the rubber as an eraser. On a few occasions, somebody would make a joke which I didn't understand, but sometimes I got the feeling the jokes were at my expense.

One day, I was playing with a hula hoop during lunchtime when a boy who was in the class below me named Karim came to me holding a basketball. He was of light skin complexion and I believe he was from Eretria. He said, 'Swap?' I dropped the hula hoop and gave him an almighty slap across his face. He initially looked stunned but then burst into tears and ran away while I carried on playing with my hula hoop. A couple of minutes later, a teacher on playground duty approached me with a sobbing Karim in tow. I had slapped him with such ferocity that I could see the hand print across the left side of his face

'Why did you hit Karim?' she asked.

I answered with an air of righteousness.

'He abused me miss, he called me 'swap'.'

'Kabia, 'swap' is not a bad thing. 'Swap' means exchange'.

Then what had happened minutes earlier made sense. Karim wanted to exchange his basketball for my hula hoop. I didn't know what 'swap' meant. I assumed he was insulting me so I took the appropriate action which was more than excessive. I felt so bad I went to Karim and rubbed his head while saying sorry. Ironically he and I became quite good friend during the rest of my time at Christ Church.

One day during my third week, I asked Thomas which religion he followed. I expected him to say he was a Christian because I assumed that all *oyinbo* people were Christians. The answer he gave to my question literally stopped me in my tracks. He said, 'I don't believe in God'. I could not comprehend what he had just said to me. I had never met a human being who did not believe in God. Back home, you were either Christian, Muslim or believed in one of the traditional gods like Orisa and Sango.

On another occasion I was sitting in the class with Thomas and Anthony when I casually mentioned something I did with my dad the day before. They all gave me a look which automatically made me feel like an outsider.

Anthony asked 'You live with your dad?

I replied, 'of course, don't you?'

'No, my mum and dad are divorced and my dad lives in Jamaica.'

Thomas said his mum and dad were also divorced but he didn't know where his dad lived. I didn't know what divorced meant but I was too proud to ask so I acted like it was not a big deal. When I got home that afternoon, the first thing I said to my mum was 'what does divorce mean'? She explained that it was when people who were married went to court to ask a judge to end their marriage. Over the next few weeks, it seemed that three-quarters of my classmates came from divorced homes. All my friends in Nigeria lived with their mum and dad, but here coming from a divorced home was not big deal. The thought of my parents divorcing was unimaginable to me.

One afternoon, approximately six weeks after I started, Miss T said she wanted to see me after school. I had a strong idea what she wanted to talk to me about. Anthony, Thomas, Dan and I had been playing tag during lunch and we did not stop when we got back into class. Miss told us to stop and take our seats but we ignored her for approximately five minutes while we continued to tag each other. When the last bell rang, I watched all my classmates including my co-culprits leave the class. They added insulted to injury by shouting 'bye Kabia' while laughing.

Miss T told me that she was very disappointed with the way I had acted in the afternoon. She said there had been a steady decline in my behaviour recently. When

I first started I was very well behaved, polite and had been a pleasure to have in her class. She had hoped that it would rub off on the rest of the class, but the opposite had happened. I had picked up the bad habits of the other kids. I was so disappointed in myself. I knew I would not have even thought about acting like I did that afternoon back at Omolewa without getting a couple of lashes. I felt like a fool, I had acted a fool to impress my friends who had left me to take the blame for everything.

Penny Sweets

... I arrived at school early one day and Dan invited me to accompany him to the sweet shop. My favourite sweet up to that point was called a Tom-Tom. There wasn't much of a variety to choose from because eating sweets was not encouraged. Whenever my dad found out that we had eating something sweet, he would make us drink *ogun Jedi Jedi.* This is a bitter concoction of herbs and roots which were meant to cleanse the stomach. I followed Dan into a very small shop which had sweets in hexagon-shaped containers on four shelves on both sides of the shop and counter at the back. I had never so many sweets in one place before in my life. While I stood there staring at the variety of colours, shapes and sizes, Dan had taken a small wicker basket and was already picking sweets of his choice. I had fifty pence, which I hoped would be enough to buy me at least five sweets. There were sweets there that I would never have been able to imagine in my wildest dream. There were some shaped like fried eggs, coca cola bottles, snakes and a long twisty rope-like liquorice just to name a few.

I picked up a basket and put some sweets in it hoping that the 50p in my pocket would be enough. I took the basket to the counter and gave it to the old lady at the till.

'How much is this please?' I asked.

I apprehensively watched her count the sweets.

'That will be ten pence please.'

'Pardon?'

'I said that will be ten pence.'

'For all of them?'

'Yes for all of them. These cost one penny each and these cost two pence each'.

In later years, whenever I heard the phrase 'like a kid in a sweet shop', I always remembered what I did after I heard the price of each individual sweet. I took the basket and rushed back where I was moments earlier, giddily gazing all around me trying to choose the sweets to buy. I decided to try everything and put one or two penny sweets from each container into the basket.

I believe I ate more sweets within four hours than in my entire eleven years even though I shared some with my classmates. The result of the biggest gorge in my life was the most intense and painful stomach ache I had ever experienced. By mid afternoon, if I had put my head any lower, I would have been sitting under the table. Fortunately Miss T took pity and asked Thomas to take me to the nurse. When we walked into sick bay it reminded me of the sick bay at Omolewa and this was state of the art in comparison. This room looked like the private hospital room I was taken to when I had malaria a few years earlier.

'What is the matter'?

He has a tummy ache Miss?' Thomas explained.

'Oh poor you.'

I tried hard to conceal my admiration of the sick bay.

'What have you eaten?'

'I ate a lot of sweets, Miss.'

With a smile and a look of compassion, she said, 'That wasn't a very good idea was it? You will be fine. Go and have a lie down on the bed.'

The bed was in a separate room and the thing that caught my eye was how neat it was.

I lay on the bed for about forty-five minutes and thought about the time I had spent in the Omolewa sick bay. It was in the school secretary's office and had a bed in the corner. On a number of occasions, I had acted as a courier for my class teacher by delivering a note to the secretary. Every time I looked at the bed, whether occupied or empty, I prayed to God that I would never have to come to the sick bay. Unfortunately I had to spend afternoon in there once and it was one of the most unpleasant experiences of my life. On this fateful day, I had started to feel unwell while getting dressed for school in the morning. I wanted to tell my dad but I was scared that he would think I was lying because I didn't want to go to school. I felt worse as the day went on but managed to get through the morning classes. It got so bad that I folded my hands on the table, rested my head on it and fell asleep on my desk. I was at the point where I did not if care I got beaten.

I felt somebody shaking me. I looked up and it was my teacher standing over me and telling me, 'go to the sick bay'. I would normally jump at any opportunity to leave the classroom but this time I was very reluctant. I wanted to decline the offer but I was too weak. 'Thank you, sir,' I said. My friend David was tasked with escorting me to the sick bay which was in another block on the school grounds. When we got there, the secretary asked in a tone devoid of concern.

'What is wrong with him?'

'He is sick, Sir asked me to bring him here.'

'OK, go and lie on the bed'.

I looked at the bed. To my disappointment but not surprise it was already occupied. The boy was a little smaller than me and he was fast asleep. I got into the bed horizontally with my face facing his feet and vice versa. I wish I could describe my time in the sick bay as tranquil, but I can't. In later years, every time I heard a typewriter being used, it reminded me of my afternoon in the sick bay. I lay on a bed which was on its last legs and a urine-smelling mattress which had been used to near destruction. While sleeping, all I kept hearing was the tap, tap, tap of the typewriters. The secretary had no regards for the patients sharing her space. I believed I would have been better off in the classroom. The phone rang constantly and people kept coming in and out. I was woken up with a sudden jolt when the school prefect rang the bell to indicate the end of the school day. I felt sweaty which was partly caused by the fever and the dream I had. I dreamt that my dad had come to pick us up but they could find me so they went home.

My experience in the Christ Church sick bay was another incident which made me thankful for being in London.

The Rush

... One day, Miss T asked me, 'Kabia can you swim'?

I felt insulted by the question.

'Yes, of course,' I replied.

I must have answered with an arrogant or aggressive tone because she looked at me sternly as if to remind me who was in charge.

'Yes, miss, I learnt to swim when I was six,' I elaborated in a more docile tone.

I omitted the fact that I had not been a pool in five years.

'Do you have swimming trunks?'

'No, miss'.

'Give this note to your parents. The class will start going swimming again every Thursday.'

That was exactly what I was hoping to hear after she asked her first question. When I got home, I showed the letter to my mum and we went to Woolworth's to buy some swimming trunks. I had learnt to swim when we lived in The Village back in Nigeria. The first few times my mum took us to the pool, I would sit and watch in amazement at how an *oyinbo* woman moved with grace and poise in the water. I was overcome with a combination of jealously, envy and admiration as she swam forwards and backwards with ease. After the first time I saw her, I made it my ambition to learn how to swim. I would say that one of the greatest ambitions of my early life was teaching myself how to swim.

Every time my siblings and I went to the pool, there would be a mad dash to be first to grab the inflatable tyre. I would always enter the pool at the shallow end with the tyre around my waist. Initially I would kick my legs as hard as possible. I then progressed to trying the breast stroke by holding onto the tyre with one hand to stay afloat and swinging my other hand in the water. Eventually I was able to swim the entire length of the shallow end without the aid of the inflatable tyre. Morufat had got the hang of the swimming before me, so I watched how she swam and copied her. She didn't move as smoothly as the *oyinbo* woman but she still moved unaided in the water and to me that was swimming. Sometimes, I would leave the house wearing just my swimming trunks, burst into a sprint when I was a few meters away from the pool and jump in without slowing down. It was the best feeling in the world. For the few seconds I was in the air, I felt totally free. I loved the rush of landing and being totally immersed in water. I also had the confidence to make my way back to the surface with ease.

The pool was drained roughly two months before we left The Village. We didn't know exactly when it was emptied but I found out in the cruellest ways possible. On the sunny fateful day, I started to sprint from the usual point and jumped in the air expecting to feel the rush of hitting the water as I had on many previous occasions. As I descended, I knew something was wrong because it was taking longer than normal to hit the water. I opened my eyes just in time to extend my legs and absorb the shock of the landing. My brain and my eyes were out of sync with each other for about 10 seconds. My eyes were showing me that there was no water in the pool, but I still felt the 'rush' of being in pool filled with water. I stood rooted to the spot I landed and looked around me hoping I was in bad dream and would wake up at any moment. I looked up and saw Moruf standing at the edge of the pool looking heartbroken. I walked around the empty pool for a while before I accepted the situation and left. Moruf and I did not say a word to each other on the long and sad walk home. I was bitter because I was not given an opportunity to have one last swim. The last few weeks in The Village were depressing.

The last time I was in a swimming pool was 1986. I had been itching and praying for the opportunity to feel the 'rush' ever since. Since I bought my swimming trunks, I walked around with a feeling that I was going to be reacquainted with a lost love. I planned how I was going impress my friends by jumping into the pool and swimming like a fresh water trout. I was going to show that African boys can swim well. On Wednesday night, I slept like a log. I dreamt of being at one with the water, doing breast and back stoke with consummate ease and being able to live underwater.

Nobody needed me to wake me up on Thursday morning. I had a bath and got dressed within fifteen minutes. I had packed my swimming trunk and towel in my bag the night before and left it at the foot of my bed. The first thing I did when I woke up was to make sure it was still there. On the way to school, I stopped to check my bag twice to ensure that I had everything I needed in there. I had been looking forward to this day for too long for it not to happen. When I got to class, I was itching to go, it seemed like Miss T was taking her time to take the register. When she finished, she said, 'who remembered to bring their swimming costume?' My hand was the first to go up. My actions must have been comical because a couple of the kids at my table began giggling. I did not care, I was about to go swimming. I looked around and people started to raise their hands nonchalantly. I could not understand why they were not as excited as I was.

Two women came into class and told us they were our swimming teachers, they said everybody should pick a partner who we would walk with to the swimming pool: 'Make sure you stay with your partner all the way until we get to the swimming pool'. I asked Dan to be my partner. We formed a line, walked through the reception and waited by the fence as we had been instructed. We waited there for what seemed like an age. I became annoyed when they gave more instructions such as, 'make sure you stick with your partner, only cross the road when we give the OK and behave yourselves'. My patience was wearing very thin, all this talk was cutting into my swimming time. I kept leaning out of the line to see why it was not moving. Then I saw the teacher walking and the first two kids started to follow her. This was it, I was about to meet my date with destiny.

The kids in front of me started to walk, I looked left, Dan started to walk and suddenly I felt a bump in my back. I felt a hand push me and heard, 'Kabia move'. I was rooted to the spot with fear. It came from nowhere and literally paralysed me for about five seconds.

I quickly wrestled myself out of the sudden paralysis and jogged to catch up with Dan. The only time I remember that happening to me was a few years previously. We had gone to our family friends the Onabajo's house for Christmas, and I was chased by a ram. Somebody shouted, '*eron ti ja o*'. A ram had got loose and everybody scattered. I stood rooted to the spot, I knew I had to run but my legs would not move. It was only when it charged me that I turned to run, I was lucky not to get gored.

I dismissed what had just happened and allowed my mind to get back to imagining all the tricks I was going to show my classmates. I told Dan and Anthony who was walking in front of me that was going to dive deep and hold my breath longer than anybody else. When we got back I was going to be the talk of the class and I couldn't wait. On the way, I noticed that Thomas was walking by himself. I was genuinely concerned because the instructions before we left was for us to make sure we walked with our partners.

'Miss, miss, Thomas does not have a partner'.

I could see from the reaction on her face that she did not understand a word I said. She looked towards where I was pointing, but could not figure out what I was talking about.

'Thomas does not have a partner,' I said again.

Suddenly she snapped at me. 'Don't worry about it, just stay in line.'

I felt like retreating into my shell like a tortoise. I was confused, I couldn't understand why she shouted at me when all I was trying to be helpful. All the excitement I was feeling seemed to evaporate. I put my head down and carried on walking. When I looked up, the area was familiar and I realised the route was the same one to my house. I became alert because if the swimming was close to my house I wanted to remember how to get there. I imagined going swimming anytime I wanted, it would be just like The Village.

At the junction where I would normally turn left, we crossed the road. A few yards further down, the line stopped in front of a massive red brick building. We waited as the teachers counted us to make sure that none had been lost on the way. I looked up at the building and saw the name in large gold plated letters: 'Seymour Leisure Centre'. I could not believe I had been walking past a swimming pool every day and was not aware of it. As we walked up the stairs, the teacher who snapped at me earlier gently pulled me out of the line to one side. She put her hand tenderly on my shoulder and bent to meet me at eye level.

'What were you trying to tell me earlier?'

I felt my heart soften as I spoke softly, 'I was trying to tell you that Thomas did not have a partner'.

'Oh OK, I am sorry I didn't hear you.'

I looked at her blankly, I didn't know what to say. I couldn't remember an adult ever apologising to me before that moment. I turned round and ran up the stairs. I took a deep breath before I opened one of the brown double doors by the gold handle and walked into a dimly-lit foyer. The line had disintegrated into small groups and I walked over to stand with Anthony, Andrew, and Thomas. The teachers were at the reception desk and I looked around eagerly for the direction of the pool. I waited for what seemed like an eternity before I heard one the teachers say, 'OK, go through the barriers to the changing rooms'.

We all walked hurriedly through the barrier as instructed and went down a flight of stairs. As I walked down, I smelt something which I hadn't smelt in five years: chlorine. I didn't know it was called chlorine then but I had never smelt it anywhere else apart from the pool at The Village. At the bottom of the stairs, the girls walked into a blue set of double doors on the right and I followed the boys through the doors on the left. I realised that I was in a changing room and taken aback by the sheer size of the room. The lockers were on three sides of three walls, and benches with inbuilt was right in the centre. I was nervous so I watched what the other boys were doing. They were all getting undressed so I began to take off my shoes and socks. Thomas pulled his trousers down and I thought that his swimming trunks looked a little flimsy. Suddenly he pulled them down and I was staring at his penis. I had never seen anything like it before in my life. Where was the round dome? He had all this extra skin which overlapped the end of the penis. Frankly, it looked deformed and it scared me a little bit. I had never seen an uncircumcised penis before. Before that day, I had seen my brother's penis, a few while I was in Omolewa and one the size of a boa constrictor at the mosque during Friday prayers. They may all have varied in size, but they all looked like mine. I did not imagine that there would be a difference between a *dudu* and *oyinbo* penis.

I tried my best to act casual and carried on getting undressed. When it came time for me to change into my swimming trunks, I wrapped my towel around my waist, took off my underpants and then put on my trunks. I put my clothes in a locker and tried to lock it but the key would not turn. I began to get frustrated, almost everybody had put their clothes in lockers and were on their way to the pool. I looked at the inside of the locker door and read 'insert 20p here'. I could not believe this was happening to me. I did not have any money on me. I looked round to see if there was anybody I could ask to borrow twenty pence or share a locker, but I was the only one left in the room. I had waited so long for this day and it was turning into a nightmare. I spent a few seconds weighing the pros and cons of leaving my locker unlocked. The lure of the swimming pool was too strong so I left the locker unlocked and I ran towards the pool.

My heart started to race with excitement and anticipation of being reunited with my long lost love. I felt nothing could stop me now.

'Kabia, Kabia wait, you have to take a shower before you enter the pool.'

I looked left and saw Andrew and Dan having a shower. I felt that there were forces working against me. I wanted to ignore them and go straight through but I was scared of what they would think of me so I went to the shower. I entered the shower area, pushed the knob and warm water came out of a nozzle mounted in the tiled wall above me. I did not understand the logic. We were going into water anyway so why get wet before entering the pool? Dan followed Anthony out of the shower and I left about twenty seconds after them. As I walked towards the entrance of the pool, I was nearly overwhelmed by the familiar smell. I heard laughter and splashing and I knew I was inches away from my goal. Walking through a short hallway, I felt I had been transported to a higher plain of existence. I had never experienced such levels of total tranquillity before.

When I finally set eyes on the pool, I was shocked by what I saw. The swimming pool was inside: it was surrounded by walls on all sides and it had a glass roof.

Subconsciously, I assumed the pool would look like the one at The Village which was outside. I stood dazed for couple of minutes as I noticed the differences. It was twice the length and width of The Village pool. It had artificial lanes created by floating dividers and there were two lifeguards sitting in their lifeguard chairs. The *oyinbo* people swimming were using three of the lanes to swim up and down the pool at different pace. I resisted the powerful urge to take a couple of steps back and taking a running jump like I used to. I saw the teachers at the other of the pool and I walked towards them. During the short walk, I was planning how I was going to enter the pool. I decided I had to impress my classmates by jumping in the air with my arms and legs stretched in the shape of a star. I imagined how impressed they would be when they saw me dive deep and hold my breath longer than they could. I had picked the spot where I begin my run and a few seconds later I would feel the 'rush'. Although the pool was noisy, I was in my own world and nobody existed in it but me.

I was two steps from the spot when I heard my name: 'Kabia, Kabia'. I looked at the direction it was coming from and it was the teacher who had snapped at me earlier. I remember thinking I would never forgive her for ruining my moment, the moment which I had been looking forward to for the past five years. I walked towards her and she then added insult to injury.

'Can you swim well?'

'Yes of course, I can swim very well.'

'Can you walk up to the point where you can swim to?'

I walked up to a point where I knew I could reach easily, but I planned to swim twice as far just to spite her.

She looked at me with some reservation but gave me the benefit of the doubt.

'OK, go on.'

This was it, I was going to finally enter the pool. I walked towards the stairs and stood there for a few seconds, looked around and exhaled loudly. I saw my classmates swimming like the *oyinbo* lady back at The Village and suddenly realised that everybody was wearing goggles. From where I was standing the pool looked twenty times bigger than when I first saw it a few minutes previously. I held on to the silver handle as I walked down the stairs leading into the water. As the bottom half of my body entered the water, the cold water nearly took my breath away. I inhaled and exhaled simultaneously to catch my breath. I was reunited with my love, my first love. After years of longing, painful daydreams, I was about to feel total freedom again. I was at total peace; fear and anxiety were banished from my body. I cupped some water in my hands and put it onto my face.

The people and noise returned. I realised I was not alone and I was pleased it was not a dream.

'Kabia, swim to where I am standing,' the teacher said.

She was standing halfway to where I told her I could swim up to. I intended to make her look stupid. I remembered how I used to be at one with the water back in The Village pool and I was about to have that feeling again. I imagined the look my mum would have on have on her face when I went through the door and told her that I had swam again.

With my heart racing, I bent my knees and submerged up to my neck. I pushed off, transferring all power to my arms which would create the initial momentum before by legs started to kick. My hands hit the water but I did propel forward as usual. My brain was sending the signals but my limbs did not want to co-operate. In fact they were working autonomously and against one another, each striving for survival. I opened my eyes, and all I saw were the blue and the tiles on the floor of the pool. I heard my hands beating the water frantically. I tried to put my legs on the floor but it seemed to have disappeared. My right leg finally connected to the floor and I was still beating the water when my left leg found safety. I found my balance, used my thumb and index finger to clear the water out of my eyes and tried to get my bearings.

I was in total disarray. This was the first time in my life that I realised my boundaries. It was a cruel feeling I had never felt before. I thought: 'this is not possible, I am Kabir. My name translates into 'The Great!' I am the son of Alhaji and Alhaja Kareem! Grandson of Chief Bello Karim and Chief Bolaji Adewummi. I have climbed the highest paw-paw and guava trees, have been stung by bees and survived an ambush by four boys at Omolewa. This is impossible'. Up until that point, I had always felt infallible.

I stood staring at the water. I refused to believe I had been rejected in such a scornful way by my first love. I had spent five years thinking about this moment and I was finding it very difficult to comprehend what had just happened.

'Kabia, Kabia, are you OK'?

I saw the teacher looking at me pityingly.

'Yes, miss, I am fine, miss.'

My embarrassment was compounded when I saw four of my classmates also looking at me. I felt like a charlatan and an unquestionable fraud. Everyone in the class was going to call me a liar and laugh at me, I would be shunned and an outcast.

I began to reason with myself. I told myself I was a little rusty, that forgetting to swim was like forgetting how to eat: impossible. I simply had to try again.

'Kabia, come out of the pool please.'

I looked at her. I closed my eyes, bent my knees and propelled myself forward. This was the first time in my life I had disobeyed a direct order from an adult. The same thing happened as before, the only difference this time was that I recovered a lot quicker. I wanted to dive under the water and disappear. Five years ago I would have been able to do it without a second thought. I saw Anthony wading through the water towards me with a look of pity across his face.

'Are you OK, Kabia'?

He put his hand across my shoulder blade.

I weakly replied, 'I am fine'.

The teacher said again, 'come out of the water please?'

I climbed out of the water feeling fragile with my dream moment shattered. I walked towards the teacher broken and defeated. I hoped she would send me to the changing room immediately so I could retreat and be alone with my humiliation.

'When last did you swim?'

I was surprised by the tenderness of her voice.

'About five years ago.'

'That is a long time, you have probably forgotten. You need to learn again. Get a float from the basket over there.'

I walked to a large metal basket with different coloured and shaped floats. I picked the biggest one

I could find, and was initially surprised about how light it was. I began to feel cold as I walked back to it teacher. It felt like everybody was looking at me. It was the exactly same feeling I had a few years before when I took the walk of shame at Omolewa. She motioned for me to give her the float and she showed me how to use it when I got in the water.

'Hold it out in front of you like this and kick your legs hard to push yourself forward through the water.'

I was consumed with fear as I walked into the pool, I had not been given time to get over my earlier shock. I stood frozen to one spot as the teacher continued to demonstrate how I should use the float. This was something I had never seen or used before. I understood the purpose when I laid it on the water and felt some resistance. I said to myself, 'Bismillahir Rahmanir Raheem'. *(In the Name of Allah, the Most Beneficent, the most Merciful)*. I took a deep breath, bent my knees and pushed forward with the float in front of me. I was surprised by how it supported my upper body in the water, but both my feet stayed on the floor.

'Don't worry Kabia, the float will keep you above the water.'

I was concentrating so hard on getting this right, I did not notice the teacher watching me. I tried it again, this time ensuring I lifted my feet off the ground. I transferred all my strength to my arms, closed my eyes and kicked my feet as hard as I could. Although still difficult, I was able to keep the top half of my body parallel with the water. Kicking was very difficult, it felt like I had cement blocks on both legs. I stopped after what I felt like five minutes quite and was proud of the minor improvement I had made. With all the effort I put into kicking, I knew I must have swum at least halfway to my initial target.

Exhausted, I looked round and was extremely disappointed to find that I was still at the same spot as where I started.

'Just carry on trying Kabia and stay in the shallow end.'

I watched her walk towards the deep end of the pool where all my classmates were. I watched enviously as Anthony dived into the water and swam towards the shallow end with consummate ease. It was then I had a realisation that although I could swim I was never a good swimmer. I thought back to my time at The Village swimming pool. When I swam, it was in quick short bursts with the aim of reaching the edge so I would have something to hold on to. I truly enjoyed the feeling of being in the water but every time I swam, it was my survival instincts which propelled me forward. I did not have any skills, my limbs did not co-operate back them either but performed their individual duties to ensure I did not drown. Anthony was swimming and enjoying it, and he hardly disturbed the water as he moved through it. The difference between us was that he was truly at one with the water and I always fought against it.

I felt a sudden weightlessness go through my body. I was being absolved of all my shame, anger, bewilderment and disappointment. I knew I would have to start all over again, but that did not make me sad. I had learnt to swim once, I would do it again. When Anthony reached the shallow end, I tried to talk to him.

'How do you float?'

'I don't know, I just do it.'

'How long have you been swimming for?'

'I don't know, probably since I was two or three.'

I took some consolation from the fact that he had been taught how to swim from an early age while I taught myself. I practiced using the float for fifteen minutes before the teacher told me that it was time to go.

I left the pool with mixed feelings of strength and exhaustion. The epiphany made me feel like I had conquered a fear that I didn't know I had. My legs felt rubbery as I walked towards the changing room. It felt like I had just used leg muscles which had been dormant for years. They were about to give way as I walked past the showers and saw a couple of my classmates having shower. I had no intention of taking another shower when I had just come out of the pool, it did not make sense to me. I sat down on the closest bench and was disappointed when I saw Anthony walking towards the shower with his towel. I didn't want to be labelled as dirty so I went to my locker to get my towel.

I grudgingly walked to the shower area and was shocked when faced with six butt cheeks, belonging to two black boys and one white. Anthony, Andrew and Thomas were stark naked with their swimming trunks on the floor. I had planned to take my shower with my shorts on like I had done earlier and I was totally unprepared for the cracks that appeared in front of me. Again not wanting to seen as odd, I slid my shorts down and stepped in the spot next to Anthony. I felt so exposed and vulnerable and tried my best to hide it. This was the first time I would be willingly naked in front of people. I stood as close to the wall as possible as I fiddled with the shower knob and stood in that same position until I built up the enough courage to turn around. When I turned around, I could not help but stare at Anthony's penis and was shocked by what I saw, it looked like Thomas's. I was more baffled than before: why would a *dudu* boy have such an ugly penis? It looked like a dried prune. I quickly composed myself, looked up and saw a bemused look on Anthony's face. He was looking intently at my penis! I can only assume he was mirroring the look I had on my face when I saw his penis. Our eyes met and we both looked away embarrassed.

Millionaire's Son

… Over time, I got closer to Dan, more so than I did with Thomas. I found Thomas to be very unhygienic. I noticed that he sometimes wore the same clothes more than two days in a row and suspected he didn't bathe regularly. I believe one of the main reasons Dan and I got close was the fact that we both came from the same country. He was born in Nigeria but came to England when he was a baby and he not been back home since then. On a number of occasions I found myself talking to him in Yoruba and only the bewildered look on his face reminded me that I was not in Nigeria anymore.

Dan asked me a thousand questions about what Nigeria was like. At that time I was quite baffled as to why he wanted to know so much about home. To me he was the luckiest kid in the world because he had been in England since he was baby. I had been dreaming about coming here since my dad told me about it when he came back from a short trip in 1984 or 85. During one of our frequent question and answer sessions, Dan asked me who my favourite musician was. I told him it was somebody called Shina Peters.

He asked me, 'Do you know somebody called Sikiru Barrister?'

I was both shocked and insulted by the question. I was shocked that he knew who this person was and insulted because he asked if I had heard of one of the biggest musicians in Nigeria.

'You mean Sikiru Ayinde Barrister. Of course I know, he is friend of one of my uncle's. How do you know about Barrister?'

'He is my dad!'

I stopped walking, looked at Dan intensely, expecting him to start laughing and confirm that he was joking. His face was dead serious. I could not believe it. I was talking to the son of Sikiru Ayinde Barrister, the Godfather of Fuji music. This kind of thing does not happen to people like me.

I wished all my friends and enemies back at Omolewa could see me now. I imagined how jealous Morufat and Moruf would be when I told them. Dan said his mum left his dad when he was two and he had never seen him since then. When I got home that day, instead of greeting my mum, the first thing I said to her was, 'the son of Ayinde Barrister is in my class'. I repeated the same statement to Morufat and Moruf as soon as they walked through the door. They were initially cynical about my claim but my excitement was so visible they eventually believed me and were nearly as excited as I was.

My first visit to Dan's house fell way short of my expectations and created serious doubts about his story. A few days after he told me who his dad was, he invited me to his house for lunch. I knew I was not supposed to leave the school ground, but this was an invitation I could not refuse. Through all my morning lessons, I daydreamed about how Dan's house would be like. Based on the videos of Barrister I had seen, I imagined he would be living in a huge mansion with Baby Benzes and sports cars parked in the front. His house was approximately ten minutes from the school but for one reason or another he was always late in the mornings. Anytime we walked near a nice looking house I expected Dan to say that it was where he lived.

While walking past a building I thought was very ugly, Dan suddenly turned and started to walk up a flight of stairs. It was a two storey council estate built in the shape of a shoe horn with red bricks. I was surprised, but I followed him up the stairs hoping that it was a shortcut to his mansion. My hopes were dashed when I saw Dan fumbling for the keys. On the second floor we walked past a few doors before we reached his door which had a 'JESUS IS LORD' sticker on the letterbox. The disappointment I felt when I saw the keys a few moments earlier could not match what I felt when the door opened. I immediately had my doubts about Dan's claims when I entered the flat. Upon entering, my first thought was, 'this is smaller than Aunty Sheri's face-me-face-you in Lagos'.

The flat did not look like it belonged to the son of a millionaire. It was a two bedroom flat with a very narrow kitchen, and a living room with a dining table crammed into it. I was in a state of disbelief for a couple of minutes before Dan introduced me to his mum. I prostrated and said 'e ka'san ma'. I assumed she was not expecting this kind of greeting because she looked at me quizzically.

'Good afternoon, how are you?'

'Fine thank you, ma,' Dan said.

'This is the new boy from my class I told you about. He is from Nigeria as well.'

'Oh OK, how is your mummy and daddy?'

They are fine ma, thank you.'

She turned to Dan and said, 'you see, this is the kind of friend you should be bringing home, not that ruffian George'.

'Mum, isn't it true that Barrister is my dad.'

I was surprised by the question but I can only assume I hid my disappointment poorly and he had seen the doubts on my face.

'Yes he is, but you haven't seen him since you were baby.'

Dan gave me a look which I took to mean: 'see, I told you'.

I followed him into his bedroom. It was about the same size as the one I was currently sharing with my brother. There was a single bed next to a wall and opposite was it a small television set. I was more jealous than surprised because I expected a kid having television in their bedroom was standard. I took a seat on the bed and looked around the room. It reminded me of the room of Kevin Arnold from my favourite TV show at the time. After eating lunch, Dan and I walked back to school in relative silence. For my part I was still wrestling with my doubts based on what I saw.

George

… I was proved right in my intuition about George's evil look after I beat him in the race. He went on to be one of the people I hated most in the world. One day, during my third week at Christ Church, I was playing with a basketball when he came towards me and said, 'give me ball'. I was surprised because he had never made any attempt to play with me since I arrived. I passed him the ball with the hope that this gesture would result in us developing a friendship. I stood there waiting for the return but he just walked away with the ball. I knew that if I allowed him to get away with this he would do it again and again.

'George, can I have my ball back please?'

'It is not yours,' he replied, 'it is for everybody'.

'But I was playing with first'.

He ignored me walked away. I jogged after him and tried to take the ball from him hand. He switched the ball over to his left hand and held me back with his right hand with surprising ease.

'Give me back my ball, give it to me.'

My attempts to retrieve my ball by force were futile, he was stronger than I expected. After a couple minutes of struggling, he dropped the ball, smiled and walked away. I was happy because I wrongly thought that I had won the battle.

Years later I realised that I had fallen into an inevitable trap, he wanted to test how strong I was and he succeeded. After this incident with the ball, things between us got gradually worse. We had quite a few more incidents before I finished at Christ Church. On one occasion he pushed in front of me in the lunch queue. While attempting to regain my rightful place, a teacher came and told me to go to the back.

'But miss, he stole my place!'

From the bewildered look she had on her face, I knew she did not understand a word I had just said. George now added insult to injury.

'He is trying to push in, miss.'

I knew this battle was lost so I meekly went to the back of the line.

A couple of weeks after my war with George started, I was sitting on the bench during lunch when I saw Karimot crying. I ran to her and asked her what was wrong. She said somebody had taken her ball. I told her to tell me who it was. When she looked round and pointed to George, my whole body filled with rage. I had purposely avoided a physical fight with this boy because I knew the chances of a win were slim, but he had had crossed the line by picking on my sister. I had to do my duty as the big brother.

I marched up to him and grabbed hold of his shirt by the neck.

'Don't touch my sister again,' I shouted.

He was so startled he dropped the ball. With one swift movement he swung me to the right. If I hadn't had a tight grip of his shirt I would have been on my back. His attempt to dislodge me from his shirt caused it to rip. By this time a small crowd had gathered.

'You ripped my shirt.'

'Don't touch my sister again or I will beat you up, you bastard.'

This was the harshest insult I knew at that time but it didn't faze him at all. As I released my grip, the first whistle was blown.

Everybody stood still as usual but I started walking towards the class 7 assembly line. When the whistle was blown the second time, everybody but George stood in their designated spot in the line. He stood right behind me and said quietly to me, 'You are going to pay for my shirt'. I ignored him but he kept on repeating the same thing while pushing my shoulder. Each time he pushed my shoulder, I got angrier and angrier.

A teacher gave our class permission to enter the building. As the line began to move I felt George try to trip me while I was walking. I continued to ignore him. He did it again while simultaneously saying, 'You are going to pay for my shirt'. When we entered the building, the line stopped moving. He pushed my shoulder again. At that moment I knew I had to fight. Tears began to role down my cheeks as I turned around and grabbed his already ripped shirt in the same spot and I pushed him against the wall.

POW, POW, he threw two jabs in quick succession.

Both landed on their target, my face, with supreme accuracy. I was dazed but still held on to his shirt.

Anthony and Dan came between us to try to and break us up.

'Anthony, tell him to let go of my shirt'.

He repeated the same sentence over and over. The more he said it the more I pulled. I knew I had lost the fight but I was determined to leave with something. I did not let the shirt go as I was finally pulled back by Dan. My tenacity with shirt-pulling caused George's torso to be exposed. Although I had lost my first fight in London, I felt I came away with a small victory because he would never be able to wear the shirt again.

I went up to the class taking two stairs at a time bypassing all the kids who were waiting patiently to enter the classroom. To observers I was crying because I had just got beaten up, but I was crying with rage because I had got into a fight which I hated. I walked in the class, sat in my chair with my arms folded and my head down and started to sniffle. The class came in without the usual ruckus, and everyone took their place. A black girl put her hand on my shoulder.

'Are you OK, Kabia?'

I managed to mumble, 'I am fine'.

Miss T came in and asked me to follow her. George was waiting outside with another teacher who was on playground duty.

'Kabia, why did you rip George's shirt?'

I could not believe what I was hearing. How she could be asking me why I ripped his shirt when he started the whole thing.

'He was abusing my sister miss, and he kicked me.'

'No, I didn't.'

'Yes you did, you are liar.'

'Stop it now, both of you. Fighting is not allowed in this school. If this happens again, I will inform your parents.'

Although I had lost the fight, I had defended my sister so ultimately it was worth it. I spent the rest of the afternoon wallowing in self-pity. By the time I got home, self-pity had given into anger and a burning desire for revenge. I didn't tell anybody about the fight when I got home and instructed Karimot not to tell anybody either. I spent most of the evening thinking of ways I could get my revenge on George. I seriously considered going to school the next day with two towels tied to my upper body. I imagined myself walking up to him and giving him two punches in the face in reciprocation. He would punch me in the stomach but I would not feel anything because of the towel. I went to bed that night angry. I dreamt about punching him in his stomach and stomping on his head with such ferocity that he would die right there in the playground.

The next morning, he was waiting for me by the gate and the first thing he said was, 'you are paying for my new shirt'. I resisted the urge to punch him in the face and walked right past him. Over the next couple of months after the fight, George and I had some verbal altercations. The reason why George hated me so much made sense when Dan told me that he considered me to be his new best friend. I asked him who his best friend was before I came to the school, he said it was George. I initially felt a sense of triumph but as I thought about it more my feelings turned to sympathy.

Guilty Pleasure

... During my eleven years, I had only ever liked one girl. She lived in the biggest mansion back in Akobo and I had seen her around a few times. I never found out her name or got the courage to talk to her. One day, her father had a garden party which I thought would be the ideal opportunity to talk to her, but alas my nerves failed me. She was even prettier up close than from afar. When I walked into the garden she began walking towards me in the opposite direction. As we walked past each other, she looked at me and said, 'hello'. My brain sent my instructions to my mouth to respond, but just not exactly what the response should be. That moment still haunts me till today. I stood on the spot like a dunce. I didn't respond and watched her walk away. I spent the rest of party putting extra effort into everything I was doing in the hope that she would notice me. I did multiple cartwheels and ran as fast I could but she didn't speak or look at me during the rest of the evening or before we left for London.

About six weeks after I arrived at Christ Church, I realised that I had started to take notice of a particular girl name Kelly. I did not pay much attention to it until the day I got an erection when I saw her walking towards me. There was no doubting it. I was attracted to this girl. As quickly as I had got excited, I was overcome with a feeling I had never experienced before and was at a loss to explain. Over the next few days, I was overwhelmed with the same mystified feeling whenever I thought of or saw her. She said 'hello' to me once and the same thing that happened in Akobo happened again. I stood on the spot looking at her like a dunce. It took me a while to figure out what I was feeling guilt and shame. I felt guilty because I was scared I was changing and shame because I liked an *oyinbo* girl. I had never thought that this would be a possibility, so I could not understand why I was feeling the way I did. Most of the girls in my class at Omolewa had short afro hair like me and I did not find any of them attractive. I thought, 'why would I come to England and like an *oyinbo* girl with hair that flowed the length of her back?'

My attraction to Kelly ended three or four weeks after it started. During that time I avoided seeing her as much as possible in a bid to reduce the feeling of shame and guilt, but I also enjoyed seeing her as well.

Dinner Guest

… One day, Anthony asked if he could come to my house after school. I was a little surprised at the request but I said yes. We were not that close at this point, but he was the most popular boy in the class and I felt privileged that he had asked to come to my house.

When we got into the lift at Landward Court, I noticed that he looked very nervous. He asked if I was sure that my mum wouldn't mind him coming over, and I reassured him it would be fine. When we entered the flat, we went straight into my bedroom, took off our coats and left them on the bed. He then asked me how he should say hello when he saw my mum. I was very surprised and impressed by his willingness to adopt my culture. I showed him how to prostrate by going towards the floor with both my hands stretched out in front of me and said, 'e ka'san ma'. He repeated this.

We then entered the kitchen where my mum was cooking. I greeted her and then introduced Anthony, she looked a little startled but stretched her hand out to shake his. Her face turned from startled to shock when Anthony prostrated and said, 'e ka'san ma'. When he rose to his feet, she still shook his hand and asked him some questions about school, his mum and where he lived. We sat in the living room watching television while my mum cooked in the kitchen. After fifteen minutes of television watching, I went to get the broom and began to sweep the living room which was part of my daily chores. I thought he might find it odd that I did not have a vacuum cleaner but he was looking at me in total amazement. He asked 'you sweep the floor'?

Of course, I reassured him that I swept the sitting room and the passage. He looked impressed as he watched me sweep. He even asked if he could try to use the broom, which we called the '*igbale*'. My mum called me into the kitchen.

'Does he know how to eat *eba*'?

I was fairly certain he hadn't eaten *eba* before, but I still went to ask him just to be sure.

'Anthony, do you know how to eat *eba*?'

'What's that?'

'It's African food that you eat with your hands.'

'OK, I will try it.'

Morufat and Karimot arrived home and set the table while Anthony and I watched TV. I became very nervous about whether he would like the food or not. Mum called out to me to say that food was ready.

We both stood up from the couch. I walked towards the kitchen and expected him to follow me. I was in the kitchen before I realised he was not behind me. I went back into the living room and saw that he was already sitting at the dining table. I gave a look of total astonishment. It took me a couple of minutes to realise why he was sitting at the table. He was expecting the food to be brought to him.

'Anthony, come and get your food.'

He looked at me embarrassed as he got up and followed me to kitchen. My sisters were already in the kitchen and had collected their plates. There were four lumps of *eba* of various sizes wrapped in clingfilm. I took one, put it on a plate and gave it to Anthony. Mum had already put the stew and meat in a bowl and I told him to take one. He looked really nervous as he took he took his food and left the kitchen.

When I got to the dining table, Morufat and Karimot were looking at Anthony curiously. This was the first time we were all about to see an English person eat *eba* and stew. He wore a nervous grin and listened attentively as Morufat demonstrated how to take a small piece of *eba*, roll it into a ball and dip into the okra stew. Mum joined us at the table and we all stared at him as he replicated what Morufat had just shown. As he put the *eba* in his mouth, he nodded his head and said, 'this is good'. We all murmured with a sense of relief and approval. I tried to study his face to see if it would betray his true thoughts, but he eagerly went for his next ball. He did not leave a single piece of *eba* on his plate. At school the next day, four people asked if they could come to my house for dinner.

Crazy New World

... I was watching the television news one day and I heard that a bomb had exploded in London. The scene looked like a disaster and sounded incredibly loud with a combination of noise from alarms and sirens from the emergency services. I was totally mesmerized by what I was watching. Things were only supposed blow up in war zones and the movies, weren't they? One statement made by the newscaster stuck with me: 'The IRA has claimed responsibility for the bombing'.

This was a whole new world to me. Why would someone want to take responsibility for bombing and killing people? Where I came from, if you commit a crime the last thing you would do is admit to it. I could not understand why people would want to kill people for no personal reason. Back home, if somebody got killed, there was always a reason. Armed robbery, political assassination, money, whatever it was, there was a reason.

It seemed that every time I watched the news in England, there was news about the IRA. By June 1992, the IRA, bomb hoaxes, the Northern Ireland troubles had become everyday words to me. After a bomb blew up, or been deactivated, a man named Gerry

Adams would usually come on TV and claim that his organisation was responsible. This was even more bizarre to me. I thought, 'was he not scared of being caught?' Whenever he was on TV, the newsreader always said, 'Gerry Adam's voice is spoken by an actor'. One day while watching BBC news with my mum, I asked why his voice was not allowed to be broadcast on TV. She said that because he was a terrorist, the Government banned his voice from being played on British TV. I thought this rule was stupid because people got to hear what he was saying, just not by his own voice.

'Why don't they just shoot him?' I said after a couple of minutes.

She looked at me and let out an almighty laugh.

'They can't do that, it is against the law.'

My confusion about the situation just became more complex. How could it be against the law for the government to shoot a known criminal? All my life, I had lived a society where military coups and political assassinations were a way of life. I had even seen armed robbers and murderers facing the firing squad while watching the news. I would say that was the day I had an understanding of the concept of 'democratic government'. Although still a little confused, I had a newfound respect for it.

Every day over a one week period in March 1992, a group of five or six from my class were taken on field trips. I was with the last group to go on the particular trip. My group took a minibus to an ugly building which turned out to be Paddington police station. We were led into a room by an *oyinbo* man who asked us to take a seat on chairs which had been arranged in a half moon.

After he introduced himself, he told us that the purpose of our visit was to learn how to report suspected packages and what to do if there was an IRA bombing. He spoke for ten minutes then split us into two groups. I was in the group with the speaker along with Thomas and another boy and the rest went with a lady whom he introduced as his 'lovely assistant'. He said he was going to show us examples of what to do if we came across a suspicious package.

We followed him down a flight of stairs which led to a massive room which was an exact replica of a London underground station platform. There was a train carriage, a train track, a bench and a phone box. My classmates and I were amazed at the level of detail. While I gawked wide eyed, Thomas and the other boy let out a big 'WOW' simultaneously. At that moment, I felt relieved that I was not the only one who was surprised at the structure. I also felt out of place because their reaction when they saw the structure was another reminder that I was in a new country and still trying to fit in. Although I spoke English better than most of my classmates, there was always new slang and mannerisms that reminded me that I was an outsider.

Our instructor asked us to look around for anything that may look out of place. We all looked around and the girl in our group shouted, 'I found something'. She was standing at the end of the platform and pointing to a bag which was on the rail line with a stick next to it. The instructor turned to us.

'What would you do in this situation?'

I put my hand in the air and he pointed to me.

'I will use the stick to get it and give it to the people who work in the station.'

'OK, go ahead.'

I thought this was the easiest test possible. We had been taught at Omolewa that it was the duty of a good student was to submit missing items to teachers so that they could be claimed by the rightful owner.

I took the stick and reached for the bag. I attempted to grab it by putting the stick through one of the handles and lifting off the track. I could feel all eyes on me as I failed at my first two attempts. At the third attempt, I managed to put the stick through one of the straps. I smiled because I thought that I would get applauded for making such a determined effort to retrieve the bag.

As I lifted it, there was a loud bang and a spark from the bag which forced me to recoil instinctively and drop the stick. The fear was only momentary, but the lesson I learnt would last a lifetime. I looked at my classmates and saw that they were as shocked as I was. We all then looked at the instructor.

'You are dead, Kabir. That was an IRA bomb. Never ever touch or try to retrieve a suspect package.'

'OK,' I said meekly.

He spoke for another ten minutes about what we should if we see an unattended package. He then looking at me directly said;

'The underground rail line was electrified and you would be electrocuted if you fell on the track and touched a rail.'

Apart from the shock of the bag blowing up, my lack of understanding why somebody would want to kill other people for no reason just grew deeper. I was very subdued as we left the building.

After we had lunch, we watched a video about the dangers of playing on the railway line. One particular scene in the video stuck in my head. It was a real-life video of some kids playing what the speaker described as 'chicken'. The kids would stand on the rail line facing a speeding train and then jump out of the way at the last second. I watched the video with sheer disbelief. I could not comprehend why anybody would risk their lives in this way. The most risky thing I had ever done was to jump on the back of a moving Peugeot pickup truck and jump off at the last minute.

The video contained about ten to fifteen scenes of kids playing chicken either by themselves or being egged by their mates. In the last scene, a train was travelling at full speed with the horn blaring and there was an *oyinbo* boy on the train track. I expected him to jump out of the way as the previous kids had done, but as the train got closer the screen went black. There was a deadly silence in the room. The video ended with statistics about how many kids are killed on train tracks every year. I did not need to shown the video or be told not to play on the train tracks. I came to the conclusion that *oyinbo* kids were crazy.

Sayers Croft

... One day in the middle of April 1992, Miss T said she had an announcement to make. She said the school had organised a trip for all Year 7 students. The bit which caught my attention was when she said it was going to be an adventure trip. I was sold immediately. I had been starved of any sort of adventure during my three months in London. I had been to adventure playgrounds, but it was nothing like going outside my front door to climb a paw-paw or guava tree in the compound. She said the class would be going to a place in the countryside called Sayers Croft.

'The trip will be a five days long and we will be staying in cabins,' she explained. 'There will be a number of activities which will include horse riding, rock climbing and canoeing, amongst other things.'

The more details she provided, the more excited I became. I rode a horse once a couple of years earlier and I had been looking forward to repeating the experience ever since. This trip was going to be my opportunity. I was abruptly jolted out of dreamland when I heard that the trip would cost £210. As quickly as I had got excited, I rapidly became deflated. £210 was a lot of money, my dad had just recently got a job and I was not confident that my parents would have that type of money.

Miss T gave out a brochure and a consent form for parents to sign. When she finished speaking, everybody started to murmur with excitement about the proposed trip. I could not concentrate for the rest of the afternoon as I fluctuated between excitement and despair. When I got home, I delayed telling my mum about the trip because I wanted to hold onto the hope for as long as possible just in case it got dashed.

I left it as late as I could and told her just before my bedtime. As she listened I could tell that she wanted me to get to the end so that she could find out how much it would cost. When I finished, she asked how much it would cost.

'It will cost £210.'

I tried to read her face to get a reaction but she gave nothing away.

'When do you have pay?' she asked calmly.

'I think in two weeks.'

'Go and ask your father.'

This statement was expected but the reason I asked her first was so that I would have an ally before I asked my dad. He worked nights and had gone to work already, so I would have to ask him when I got back from school the next day.

That night, I dreamt about riding the horses, climbing ropes and playing games. It was going to be the best opportunity to re-ignite my sense of adventure which I had always taken for granted while in Nigeria. During the morning break the next day, I asked Dan, Anthony and Thomas whether they were going to go on the trip.

Thomas said he would not be going, Daniel said he hadn't asked his mum yet and Anthony said his mum had already given him the money to pay for himself and his twin brother Andrew. I was so jealous of Anthony. Three or four people asked me over the course of the day if I would be going on the trip and I was forced to tell them I didn't know yet.

When I got home that afternoon, my dad was sleeping. I sought Morufat's advice on the best approach I should take when asking my dad for the money for the trip. She suggested that I should prepare by doing a roleplay in which she took on the role of our dad. It went quite well, I spoke about the trip with confidence and Morufat was on point with her 'uh huh, uh huh' and expected questions such as 'when is it and how much will it cost?'

I waited patiently and he woke up for work around 8pm. I had a ninety minute window to ask him for what I needed or I would have to wait until the next day. He sat in the sitting room while I built up my courage by pacing up and down the corridor. After two aborted attempts, I took a deep breath and walking through the living room door. Unfortunately my nerves failed me again. I pretended I was looking for a book and promptly walked back out. I paced the corridor a few more times before I finally acquired my courage and walked into the living room to do what needed to be done.

I opened the door and walked in slowly. He was sitting on the edge of sofa watching the news.

'Daddy?'

As soon as he turned round to look at me, I wanted to run out of the room, but I knew that if I didn't ask the question now, I could kiss Sayers Croft goodbye.

'There is a trip at school that I want to go on.'

One thing I knew that he hated was when people mumbled when talking to him, so I had to be clear and concise. He had declined requests on previous occasions because the pitch was not delivered articulately enough.

'The trip is going to be for one week and we are going running, horse riding and rowing'.

'Uh huh, uh huh, when is it?'

I knew where this was going. Requests had also been denied because they were not asked within a sufficient time frame.

'It is in four weeks.'

He huffed and scratched his head simultaneously. He didn't say anything for about a minute. I stood submissively with my hands behind my back while he stared at the television. Then the inevitable question came.

'How much will it cost?'

'It is going to cost £210'.

'Whhaat!!! Two hundred and ten pounds for what? What are you going to do for £210?'

I wanted to run out of the living room but I stood rooted to the spot. With his elbow on his knee and his forehead in the palm of his right hand, he shook his head and kept repeating 'two hundred and ten pounds' with a murmur of anguish after each repetition.

At this point, I had already thought of the lies I was going to tell my friend as my reason for not going on the trip.

'Go and ask your mother,' he said.

'I have asked her already, she told me to ask you.'

He shot me a look in anger, maybe because he had been outmanoeuvred and he would look like the bad guy if he said no.

'OK, leave it with me I will think about it.'

It was a better answer than I was expecting. I understood that 'I will think about it' meant there was a 50-50 chance, he would say yes.

'But if you put one foot wrong between now and the time I make up my mind, then it is a definitely no.'

I told Morufat how it went and then stayed in my room until my father went to work. I didn't want to risk doing something wrong which would then give him the perfect reason to say no. At school the next day, I looked on enviously as more of my classmates paid for the trip and prayed that nobody asked me if I was coming or not.

I got home around 4pm feeling tense and apprehensive. I knew dad usually woke up around 7:30pm and he would wait until the last minute before giving me an answer. It was my turn to sweep the passage and wash the plates so I made sure I completed my chores as promptly and efficiently as possible.

When he woke up, I tried to gauge his mood in hope it would give me a clue. He watched television, ate his dinner and got ready to go to work. He didn't even give an indication that he had thought about the previous evening's conversation. I was in a miserable mood all evening. When he was putting on his work clothes and boots, I accepted that my misery would continue for at least another day. I watched him put on his coat and walk out of the front door. As soon as it closed I started crying and went to my bedroom. I cried under the duvet for about ten minutes when I heard my mum calling me. I wiped my eyes and went to the sitting room.

'*Se o nsukun ni.*'

'No I was not crying.'

I knew she didn't believe me, but she didn't push it. She sat next to me.

'I have spoken to daddy about your trip, and he said you can go.'

A combined feeling of relief and elation went through me like a bolt of electricity. I hugged her tightly and kept kissing her on the cheek while repeating 'thank you'.

She told me about the discussion they had regarding the trip. He agreed to pay the majority if she paid the rest. I went to sleep on a high and woke up with the same level of elation. I could not wait to get to school. If Karimot wasn't walking with me, I think I would have ran all the way there. When I saw Dan, the first thing I said was, 'my daddy said I can go to Sayers Croft'. He was a lot happier than I expected. He gave me half a hug before enthusiastically rushing over to Anthony, 'Kabia is coming with us on the school trip'. Anthony looked at me, gave me thumbs and said, 'that's good'.

During the morning registration, before she even asked if anybody else would be going on the trip, I told Miss T that my parents had given permission for me to go.

'OK Kabia, can you bring the permission slip and the money on Monday please?'

It seemed that now that I was going on the trip, everybody was talking about it. The day flowed seamlessly, the only negative thoughts occurred when I thought about how I would have to go through the whole weekend without doing something which would upset my dad, thus giving him a valid reason to punish me by taking the trip away from me. On the way home, I made plans to stay out of trouble over the weekend and also impress my father. I would do my chores as soon I as I woke up, make my parents tea and take it to them while they were still in bed. I would say my morning prayers at around the same time my dad was getting out of bed. I wouldn't fight with Karimot and I would do everything that is requested of me promptly.

The only flaw in my plan was that any transgression I had committed previously but had not been caught could be discovered in the weekend. This could lead to the cancellation of the trip as punishment. As soon as I opened the front door, I had a feeling that something was wrong. The flat was usually quiet but there was an eerie silence this afternoon. I put my bag in my bedroom and then went to Morufat's room. As soon as I saw her, the look on her face confirmed that something was wrong.

'Ki lo nsele' *I asked.*

'Alhaja Mummy ti kú' my sister replied.

I felt like three grown men had punched me in the stomach simultaneously. I didn't really know my grandmother well but the news of her death shook me to my core.

Sadly, I could only remember two occasions when I spent time with her in my mind. The first was when I was around six or seven years-old. She had come to stay with us for a couple of weeks during the summer holidays. One day, I heard someone shouting '*ole ole*'. I went to investigate the ruckus and I was shocked to see my grandmother shouting at Morufat. I couldn't understand why she would be accusing my sister of stealing her clothes and going to sell them in the market. Bewilderment quickly turned to anger when I saw my sister visibly upset, but my dad was trying to placate my grandmother. I remember thinking he should be defending his daughter, not trying to make this old woman happy. The whole event became even more confusing when later on in the day I saw her talking to Morufat in a very gentle and tender manner like they were best friends.

When my mum came back from work that day, I distinctly remember her talking to Morufat and she said '*o se*' (thank you). My mother explained to her that my grandmother didn't know what she was doing. That event only made sense to me years later when my mother explained that my grandmother suffered from Alzheimer's. The pain and sorrow I felt after I heard of my grandmother's death was for my mother. I knew she would be in pain and I could not think of anything I would be able to do to soothe her pain.

I walked to her bedroom and pushed the door open tentatively. For the second time in six months, I saw my mum crying and there was nothing I could do. I went and sat on the bed next to her and gave her a hug. It was all I could do. Everybody was subdued for the whole weekend. My mum spent a lot time on the phone with Aunty Sheri in Nigeria trying to get information on the funeral which was happening on the Saturday. I could see that she was hurt that she was not able to be there at the funeral. That was when the negative aspect of being so far away from home dawned on me. The moment I realised the personal implications of my grandmother's death was the most traumatic of my life up until that point.

On Saturday, the day of funeral, I was in my sisters' room sitting on Karimots' bed and talking to Morufat about what was going on back home. The conversation drifted to the expense of the trip and how much the funeral would cost. She was concerned that my mum and the other siblings in America would be expected to bear the brunt of the cost because they were abroad. I suddenly remembered my trip to Sayers Croft. I hadn't thought about that since I walked through the front door the day before.

'Do you think there will still be money to pay for my trip'?

The look Morufat gave me was one of disgust. I was disgusted with my own selfishness but I could not help myself, I had to ask. At that moment I knew I would not be going on the trip. It felt like I had been hit by a locomotive train travelling at full speed. I imagined how I would have to tell my friends that I would no longer be coming on the trip. I was afraid they would call me a liar and would not want to play with me anymore.

I went to my bedroom for solitude. The tears started to recede after about ten minutes. Then I started to imagine Dan and Anthony riding horses and all the other activities I would miss out on and the tears started to flow again. I seriously contemplated going to ask my mum if I could still go on the trip, but when I saw her I knew that my selfishness could add to the pain she was already in. I knew that if I asked, she would not want to disappoint me, but then I would never forgive myself.

The rest of the weekend went by in a blur. We all helped my mum pack her suitcases and basically tried to stay out of the way as much as possible. I spent the rest of the weekend wallowing in self-pity and tried to formulate a credible story to tell my friends. On Monday morning, before going to school, my dad called the family together to say a short prayer because my mum was travelling later in the evening. I hugged her as tightly as I could. I hated it when she left us to come to London and I was not expecting her to leave us again so soon to complete the reverse journey.

The walk to school that morning was agonising. Half an hour before school started and I had not come up with a credible story. Immediately after Miss T finished calling the register, I went to her desk.

'Miss, I will not be going on the trip again.'

I turned around and sat back at my desk. I felt that I had to do that because if I had attempted to tell her the reason why I was not going, I would start to cry right in front of the whole class. By first break, I had failed to think of a suitable lie, so while going on first break I spoke to Dan.

'I cannot go on the trip because my grandmother died and my mummy has to go home.'

'OK, sorry Kabia.'

I was relieved that he didn't ask for any elaboration and I found I didn't care if he believed me or not. Telling my teacher and Dan seemed to lift a huge weight off my shoulders. Although I was still disappointed about missing out of the trip I slowly accepted that it was not going to happen.

Just not Cricket

... The week prior to the Sayers Croft trip was horrible. The class had split into two camps: those going on the trip and those staying behind. On Monday morning those going on the trip showed some discretion during their discussions out of sympathy for those of us staying behind. By Wednesday afternoon, however, their discretion had been replaced by unadulterated joy.

That morning, the chaperones for the trip had come into our class and asked the Sayers Croft group to make their way into the assembly hall. My camp looked on enviously as they filed out of the classroom. There were eight of left behind. A few minutes later, the Headmaster, Mr Lynch, came into the class room. He rubbed his palms together.

'Right those of you not going on the trip, we have made some plans for you so that you won't totally miss out.'

He told us that two day trips had been arranged for us and we were to attend Year 6 classes for the three days we would be in school. He described the day trips with a vigour which made me feel little better about not going on the main trip. He made us feel like our camp was going to have the most fun and the other camp were the ones who were going to miss out.

Our camp was going to have a picnic at Hyde Park, then go to Paddington train station to draw trains and take a walk by a canal. I felt a lot better than I did few minutes previously. When he left the class, I looked round and saw joy on the faces of my camp and a sense of elation filled the room. Without speaking to each other, we seemed to have formed a siege mentality of us against them.

That mentality was broken a few minutes later when the other camp came into the classroom all in a hysterical state of excitement. I longed to be in the other camp as soon as I heard someone say, 'this is going to be wicked'. They all had permanent grins on their faces. The afternoon was torture, as I was the only person on my table that wasn't going on the trip. I felt insignificant as my table mates discussed the activities they had been told they would be performing.

'Have you ever ridden a horse'?

'They said we are going to go camping and rock climbing.'

I was forced to listen jealously as these questions went back and forth for the rest of the day.

By Friday afternoon, I felt totally invisible. This time the chaperones didn't bother using the sports hall for the last minute meeting. They had it in the classroom as those who weren't going looked on enviously. I took solace in the fact that a small group of us were going to have our own mini-adventure but deep in my mind I knew I would give my right arm to be on the coach on that Monday morning.

Over the weekend, I made my peace with the fact that I was not going on the trip. By Sunday night, I was actually looking forward to the week ahead. From the Friday meeting, I knew that the coach was supposed to depart at 7:30am. My heart sank when I got to school at 8:30 and everybody was outside with their parents and suitcases. The jealously and resentment made a swift return. I felt that God was punishing me for something I had done wrong previously. I was hoping they would have left by the time I arrived at school, but I had to walk past my classmates into the playground. I stood by the fence and looked on as they entered the coach and waved to their parents as it pulled away. I felt a sense of relief when the coach turned around the corner.

The silence in the classroom that morning was deafening. I realised that the only person I really spoke to was Thomas. Although I had been assigned to Year 6 classes on Monday and Tuesday, I spent most of my time in the library.

Wednesday morning arrived. I made a bread and butter sandwich for my packed lunch, and I took an apple from the fruit bowl and bought a Ribena drink on the way to school. Around 10am, we all met at the reception as we had been instructed the day before. Our chaperone walked into the reception.

'Right, we are going to Paddington station today to do a bit of train spotting and as a surprise Mr Lynch will be coming with us.'

'Train spotting' was not a term I had ever heard but I was able to deduce that we would be looking at trains.

'Have you all got your pencils and drawing paper?'

I said, 'Yessss!!!'

Everyone laughed! She asked the question in a way which I perceived required an enthusiastic response from the group. I was the only one who responded which was quite embarrassing, but it seemed to break the ice amongst the group.

On the way to the station, everyone paired off and I began talking to an Indian boy. I had a play fight with him during my second week at the school, but we did not interact again until that morning. Walking into Paddington station reminded me of the day we arrived in London, it looked like an airport. Men in suits carrying briefcase were walking swiftly in all directions and there was a new announcement over the tannoy every two minutes. We followed our chaperone to the last platform in the station. We walked past numerous stationary trains, and four empty tracks. The trains were a lot bigger the ones we had used on the London underground.

When we reached the last platform, I was faced with the biggest machine I had ever seen my life: a giant locomotive. 'Wow', the group said in unison. I was shocked when I realised I said 'wow' instinctively. I was happy and sad with equal measure. I was happy because for the first time since my arrival, I was not an outsider. On the other hand, I felt I was slowly losing my African identity.

We were instructed to find a place to sit on the floor and start drawing whatever we wanted. I was a very poor artist and I became nervous. I told my new Indian friend that I had decided to draw the front of the locomotive. He chose to draw the platform we were standing on with the locomotive as well. I sat down on the cold marble floor, and stared at the locomotive for a few minutes just so to appreciate its magnificence.

We spent about an hour drawing before we formed a circle to eat our lunch. I sat down between my Indian friend and an *oyinbo* girl. We felt special eating lunch on the platform. I was happy because I would have a story to tell the others who went to Sayers Croft trip when they returned the next week.

'Do you want some cheese?'

The *oyinbo* girl next to me was offering part of her lunch which was a piece of cheese. I had never tasted cheese before and I wanted to decline, but I didn't want to be rude so I accepted. I slowly unwrapped the red foil paper and looked inquisitively at the triangular-shaped cheese with a peculiar smell. I took a small bite and immediately spat it into my hand. I thought, 'this girl is trying to poison me'. I had never tasted anything so disgusting in my life. I could not comprehend how something that tasted so awful could be considered food. I drank the carton of Ribena in one gulp to try to get the taste out of my mouth. I scraped my tongue using my upper teeth and used my forearm to wipe my mouth vigorously. My actions must have been very comical because everyone in the circle, including the chaperone, was laughing hard. I did not find it funny. That moment scarred me for life. I have not eaten raw cheese since that day.

After lunch I went back to my paper to complete my drawing. On a couple of occasions, my mind wandered to what the others were doing at Sayers Croft at that particular time.

'Fifteen more minutes please', said the chaperone.

I looked at the big clock on the platform and was surprised that it was quarter past two. I was very happy with the outcome of my drawing, I felt it was the best drawings I had ever done up to that point in my life.

On the way back to school I was so engrossed in conversation with my Indian friend that I did not realise that we were taking a different route. I was pleasantly surprised when I saw the first boat. We were walking by a canal. I stopped walking and stared. It was long, colourful and magnificent. I was in for more shocks when I looked up and saw long boats as far as the eye could see, moored on both sides of the canal. I had never seen anything like it in my life. By the time I composed myself, the group were quite a few metres ahead. I hastened my step to catch up with them and stopped when I reached Mr Lynch.

'Why are there so many boats on the river, sir?'

He didn't hear what I had said the first time, so he bent down a little and put his hand on my back.

'Say that again?'

' Why are the boats on the river sir?'

'People live in them?'

'Pardon?'

'Yeaaah, people live in them'.

I wanted to ask more questions - like how was that possible and why would anyone want to live on a boat? - but I was too shocked to talk.

The walk along the canal is one of my earliest memories of feeling total serenity. It caused my thoughts to wander to Omolewa. I couldn't imagine this just six months ago, when I was playing with a patched football on gravel and hustling to get a quick turn on the swings. Now I was walking down a canal which had boats that people lived in permanently. I stopped to look in admiration as a canal boat went past us. The person driving it saw and waved at us. Mr Lynch and I waved back. He looked at me.

'You know I requested that boat to come past at exactly twenty past three,' he said.

He and the chaperone chuckled, but I was awed at the fact that Mr Lynch had arranged for the boat to go past at this time purposely for our benefit. It was not something that could ever be happen in Nigeria. This confirmed a subconscious thought about *oyinbo* being superior to *dudu*. It was not until years later, after some retrospective thought that I realised that he was joking. It was my earliest experience of English humour, some of which still eludes me until today. The events of the day had exceeded my expectations. One regret I had later is that I did not keep hold of my drawing. I felt that it was one of my greatest accomplishments during my time at Christ Church and would have served as a reminder of a wonderful day.

Thursday started off well. On the way to school, I had decided that I would go straight into the class. I felt there would be no point going to the playground because my usual playmates would not be there. I was surprised when I found out that I was not the only person who had the idea. The majority of my camp was already in the class sitting on one table. I was genuinely happy to see them which I found a little odd. I took my place at the table and we started talking about the previous day's event.

Five minutes before the bell went, our chaperone came into the classroom and was taken aback when she saw all of us already in our seats. The look on her face made everyone laugh. When she settled, she started to talk about what had been planned for the day. She told us that in addition to the picnic at Hyde Park we were also going to play a game of cricket. Yesss!!! This was repeated simultaneously by everybody. Some clapped and I instantly gave my Indian friend a high five, which again troubled me immediately. I had never played cricket before so I didn't understand why I was getting excited. I had seen other kids playing but I had never played myself.

Our chaperone said she would be giving everybody tasks to assist with the preparation of the trip. My task would be to get the cricket equipment from the equipment room. I was proud because I had been given the most important responsibility and I was eager to carry it with military precision. I went to the sports room, gathered all the equipment and put it into the cricket bag. When I got back to the classroom, the chaperone addressed me.

'Did you pack everything Kabia? The bat stumps and balls?'

With confidence I replied, 'Yes miss'.

The walk from school to the park took approximately forty-five minutes and I shared carrying the cricket equipment with my Indian friend. When we reached the park, we settled at a spot where Mr Lynch had chosen and it was decided that we should start the cricket game after lunch. Most of the others went off to play hide and seek but I decided to stay at the spot.

As I sat down, the heat from the sun rays took me on another nostalgic journey back to Omolewa. I thought deeply about the friends I had left behind and wandered if they missed me at all. I always imagined that when term resumed everyone in my class would ask where I had gone and there would be a big commotion when they found out I had gone to London. I dreamt of walking back to the school and everyone would come out to look at the boy who had just returned from London. I would regale them with stories of what London was like, my friends would love me and my enemies would hate me because I was somebody.

I suddenly felt someone tap me on my shoulder.

'Are you OK, Kabia?'

It was at that moment that I realised that my life was changing forever. I accepted that it was very unlikely that I would go back to Omolewa or see my friends again. The chaperone was standing over me. I looked up.

'Yes miss, I am fine.'

I joined my friends playing hide and seek, and joked and laughed with them. For the first time since I arrived I did not feel like the new African boy, I was just one of the kids. The day was perfect.

After lunch we gathered to start the cricket game. I was the first to raise my hand when Mr Lynch asked who wanted to be captains. When the teams had been selected, I took the stumps out of the cricket bag and began to set up the blue plastic cricket stumps with my Indian friend.

I will remember the next few moments for the rest of my life. I was laughing as I was putting the second stump into the base when I heard the teacher speak to me loudly.

'Kabia, you forgot the cricket bat.'

I felt my heart stop beating and I suddenly felt very cold. I closed my eyes and pictured the blue cricket bat on the shelf in the store room. At the time, I was not to know that this would be one the most significant moments in my life.

At Omolewa, I was used to not being the brightest, the strongest or the most popular. I had failed a few exams, came last in a number of races and was used to being one the last few to be picked for football games. None of these experiences prepared me for the feeling of total and abject failure which engulfed me at that moment. I have never totally recovered from the trauma of feeling utterly worthless and don't believe I ever will. Subsequently, throughout my life since then, when I have been unsuccessful at something or let somebody down, I always relived this experience. It became a symbol of personal failure which I have carried with me since that sunny day in May 1992.

When I opened my eyes, I saw Miss holding the empty cricket bag with the same look my mum gave me when I did something wrong. I looked around me and all the kids were looking at me. The looks on their faces epitomised how I felt: disgust. I had been purposely humiliated for wearing dirty socks in front of a whole school of about three hundred kids, but at least I was part of a group and the humiliation was shared. This time I was exposed. There was nowhere to run or hide. The silence from these eight individuals was louder than three hundred kids shouting, 'shame, shame, shame'. I had single-handedly ruined everybody's day and felt like a pariah.

I could feel the tears formulating.

'I am sorry, miss. I forgot it on the shelf.'

She stood silently staring at me for a few moments which felt like hours.

'Don't worry, we will just have use one of the stumps.'

In a split second, the mood in the group had changed. We all knew that it would not be the same without a cricket bat. Mr Lynch batted first to show that it was possible to use the stump instead of a bat. The first ten minutes was tense, slow and dull, but after that the difficulty of hitting the tennis ball with the stump seemed to make the game more challenging and interesting.

Twenty minutes into the game, they were having fun again. They had adapted to the situation and were enjoying themselves tremendously. Although things seemed to have turned out well, I was still overwhelmed with guilt. As a self-imposed punishment I decided that I would not enjoy myself for the rest of the afternoon and even in this I was unsuccessful. I thoroughly enjoyed myself.

After the game, I was surprised when the chaperone told me to pack up the equipment. My confidence was at rock bottom because I was scared of making another mistake. I packed all the cricket equipment very carefully and searched the area four times to ensure that I did not leave anything behind. When we got back to the school gate, I walked hastily to the store room. The first thing I saw even before putting on the lights was the cricket bat on the shelf as I had remembered during that horrible moment in the park. I picked it up and looked at it for about five minutes as if to conquer the source of my greatest failure.

On Monday morning, the classroom returned to its normal size. The Sayers Croft camp had returned and I wanted to slap each and every one of them in the face. The atmosphere was worse than the week before they went on their trip. They were talked non-stop about what they did on the trip. I grew jealous as Dan and Anthony described riding horses, rock climbing, canoeing and night camping. I decided not to tell any of them about my camp's excursions. They felt pale in comparison to what they were describing.

Just when I thought the depths of my torment couldn't sink any further, Miss T announced that we would be watching a video of the Sayers Croft trip. My curiosity surpassed my jealousy and I repositioned my chair to get a better view of the TV. The video was about ten minutes long, and it started by showing everybody on the coach on Monday morning. I could see the exhilaration and anticipation of the adventure ahead. I watched them being taught how to ride horses. I watched them being fitted with helmets and climbing gear as they abseiled on an artificial rock. I watched them climb on rocks with a spectacular waterfall behind them, and also canoeing.

When the video ended, I was happy for my friends because I could see that they enjoyed themselves thoroughly. Watching the video allowed me to share in the adventure which I genuinely appreciated. The trip was the main source of conversation for the rest of the day. I asked Dan and Anthony how the trip was and they both said it was 'wicked'. During the rest of the week, everybody went back to their respective camps. I did not talk to or play with the Indian boy I had befriended for the rest of the school year.

This was the last significant event during my time at Christ Church. I felt I had adapted well to London during my first five months. It was by far the most exciting period of my life up to that point. I experienced things I had only seen in movies, and saw things I had dreamed about for years. I sat my SAT exams in June 1992 and started applying for secondary schools.

Odun Ile Ya

… Our first Eid Kabir celebration in London took place in June 1992. The differences between this and the previous six or seven I could remember were substantial. Amongst other things, it served as poignant reminder that I was in a foreign land and it made me yearn my motherland more than any time since I arrived. I began to feel homesick a couple of days after my mum told me when the date of Eid Kabir would fall. All my life, the preparations before Eid were more fun than the day itself. With my single-minded desire to come to London, I did not have the foresight to appreciate what I would be leaving behind until the realisation was forced upon me. I woke on the Saturday morning filled the same excitement that always accompanied this day. This feeling amplified because this was the first time in two years that my mum would be with us on Eid. There was a collective joyfulness in our flat because it felt like old times because my family was complete.

I felt special yet inconspicuous as we waited at the bus stop with mainly Arab people. I saw a few people looking at us inquisitively, probably because of my parent's African outfits, but the majority didn't care. It wasn't a big deal to them that it was Eid-Kabir, they were going about their business. The bus was packed with people making their way to the mosque for prayers. Although I was amongst fellow Muslims, I still felt uneasy, probably because we were the only black people on there.

I knew we were close to the mosque when the traffic began to build up and I saw crowds of people in Muslim attire walking in the same direction. The bus driver opened the doors before the official bus stop and we got off and joined the crowd. I felt good but there was still something missing. When we arrived at Regent's Park mosque, we agreed a spot for us to meet after the prayers.

My mum and my sisters went towards the women's section while Moruf and I followed my dad towards the men's section. The courtyard of the mosque was filled to the brim with people already seated. We carefully negotiated our way through them to go and perform our ablutions. As I did my ablutions, I felt I was under scrutiny from the intense looks I was getting from the Arab and Asian men. When we all finished, we were directed out to the courtyard because there was no space inside. We were able to find spaces to sit close to each and offered our two customary rakat prayers. I listened to the sermon but quickly lost interest because it was in Arabic which was not translated into English. As I listened to the soothing and beautifully recited Quranic verses, I began to reminisce how we celebrated this day back home.

Back in Nigeria, we would know that Eid-Kabir was close when dad brought home a ram three to four weeks before the date and then a second one a week later. These first rams were for my grandparents who lived in Lagos and would be delivered to them a week before Eid. In 1989, he bought a ram two months before the Eid. My siblings and I began to develop affections him. The ram would meet us at the gate when we returned from school and when set loose he would wander around the neighbourhood and return before sunset. He was, unofficially, our pet. I was surprised by how sad we all were when he was loaded into the Volkswagen Beetle for the trip to Lagos. We all knew what fate awaited him. I briefly considered asking my dad if he could be spared, but I knew what the response would be.

After the first ram had been delivered, he would either buy another one on his return from Lagos or a week afterwards. Every time he went out, we hoped it was to buy the ram. When he returned, we would rush to go and meet him by the car to see if he had bought our own ram. The first one of us to reach the car would shout, '*daddy ti ra eran*'. This was to inform the others that the ram had been bought. I would always look at my father with a great deal of respect as he unloaded the ram from the car.

A couple of weeks before the big day, my mum would take us to the tailor to have us measured for our *Aso odun*. Eid-Kabir was a national holiday so there was no school which made the day even more special. We would all be awake by 7am, then we would go and collect our *Aso odun* from our parent's bedroom and be in the car by 8am. When my mum was home, we would take two cars, with the girls going with my mum and us boys going with my dad.

As soon as we drove out of our front gate, the celebratory atmosphere was almost tangible. There would be families at the bus stop in their best *Aso odun*, some with their sacrificial goats or rams. Others would be walking on the side of the road on their way to or from the mosque. Some houses would have started their cooking for the day. We always went to our local mosque on the grounds of University of Ibadan.

On one occasion we were running late and my dad was forced to hastily park the car on the express road and join the group of worshippers who were praying on the side of the road. As we drove through the gates, we would see hundreds of people on one side of the road returning from the mosque and on the other side were people on their way to the mosque.

The sermons would be recited in Arabic and then translated into Yoruba, all of which became boring after a while. As much as I enjoyed going to the mosque, this was a prelude to the main occasion. After prayers we would meet by the car and as we drove out, it would be surrounded by hawkers selling a variety of goods ranging from Qurans and prayer beads to sandals and wristwatches.

When we arrived home, the real fun would begin. My dad would have arranged for an Imam to assist with the slaughter of the ram and some of the workers from the farm to do the cooking and cleaning. Without fail, the movie *The Message* would be shown on TV. I must have watched that movie six or seven times. It was special to me because it told the story of the birth of the Islamic faith. I didn't fully understand it but I loved the battle scenes. When it was time for the slaughter of the ram, the Imam would skilfully grab the ram's legs, force it to the ground and then tie the two hind legs and one of the front legs together with rope. I always felt a great sense of pride towards my father when I watched him cover the eye of the ram with its ear.

He would say, '*Bismillahir Rahmanir Rahim*'. Then he put the knife to the throat and slaughtered the animal which would be thrashing vigorously. No matter how many times I saw a ram or goat being slaughtered, I always felt a fleeting sense of pity. The blood flowed into a pre-dug hole or into the gutter, and after a few minutes the thrashing would stop. The corpse would be left for about twenty minutes to ensure that all the blood drained out of the body. The men would get ready for the real work to begin by stripping down to their trousers. The same piece of rope used to tie the legs would be tied tightly at the neck and just below the knee of one of the hind legs. Air was blown into a tiny cut made above the knee which gradually inflated the stomach. The blower would hit hard with a clenched fist at regular intervals to ensure that air was not escaping. The carcass would be washed with a bar of bath soap and the hair scraped off with a shaving razor. An incision was then made on the hairless underbelly, the intestines extracted and given to the women to prepare. The meat was then butchered into smaller pieces with a collection of knives and cutlasses. The Imam usually received a large part of the thigh in addition to payment which was part of our Zakat (giving to charity).

This whole process took anywhere between ninety minutes to two hours from start to finish. I would watch the process with the same sense of marvel every time. By 3pm, the house would be filled with our Christian friends. Most would stay for only a couple of hours because they had to visit their other Muslim friends across the city. Food and drink was plentiful and by the end of the day, I would be exhausted from playing with my friends all day.

Back in the Regent's Park mosque, I came out of my reflective state when everybody stood up in one swift motion to begin the prayers. I lost my dad and brother temporarily in the shuffle to fill the empty spaces for the two Rakat prayers. After the prayers, we miraculously found the girls amongst thousands of people trying to leave the mosque.

'Right, shall we go to Kentucky Fried Chicken?' asked my mother.

We all agreed almost simultaneously with the same level of delight.

While on the bus 274, Morufat began to take pictures with her camera. Seeing the joy on my family's faces made me appreciate this day a little bit more. Although the bus was full, they looked free and content. We got off at Marble Arch and I began to salivate as we made our way to the Kentucky Fried Chicken restaurant. There were long lines at all the tills so my mum told Karimot and I to follow my dad to find a place for us to sit. She said the rest of them would order the food and bring it over to us. We found a booth big enough for six and settled in. While waiting for our food, I took a long look at my father and realised that he had put on a little weight since we arrived. He asked us softly if we were enjoying ourselves and we both responded, 'yes daddy'. This rarely seen soft side he exhibited reminded me of something that happened during the Eid-Fitr (celebration at the end of Ramadan) celebration two years previously in Nigeria.

My father would usually buy a small goat for to slaughter a week before the big day. My siblings and

I were worried and disappointed when he hadn't bought the animal a day before Eid-Fitr. When my dad returned from the farm, Morufat and Moruf decided it would be best for me to ask him if he intended to buy the customary goat. I walked into the living room and found him slouched on the chair looking totally drained. I summed up the willpower and said, 'daddy, when are you going to buy the goat for Eid?' He gave me a look which I had never seen before and would not decipher until years later: it was a father's desire not to disappoint his children. He puffed out hard and spoke softly.

'Okay, okay, I will buy it.'

'Thank you, daddy'.

A wide smile appeared across his face as I turned to leave the sitting room. He went out and returned a couple of hours later with a brown goat.

During conversations with my mother years later, I found out that things were financially difficult during that period, so buying a goat was probably not high on his list of priorities. I was happy when he bought the goat but I did not appreciate its significance till years later when I realised he probably had to find the money just to make his children happy.

Morufat Eid-Kabir 1992

Moruf Eid-Kabir 1992

In Kentucky Fried Chicken, the others returned with the food. I saw a few *oyinbo* people looking at my mum's native outfit. She carried herself with a grace and charm I always admired. It was then I began to appreciate the uniqueness of the situation I was in. I was celebrating Eid-Kabir in London with just my family. As much as I missed the big celebrations back home, the simplicity of this celebration was what made it so special. Everyone looked so happy, this was when I realised that I would be happy anywhere in the world as long as I was with my family.

The Cinema

… Visiting the cinema became one of my top five things to do in London. My desire to watch a film in a cinema was awakened when I was about seven or eight years old and my mum told me about her frequent trips to the cinema when she was a student nurse in London. I had never been to cinema before in my life, and the first and only previous attempt to see a film on the big screen had ended in bitter disappointment.

It was 1990 and my mum was back home from Saudi Arabia. The only cinema that I knew about in Ibadan was at the television station which was about 20 minutes from our house. The trip to the cinema was meant to be compensation for an earlier outing that failed to materialise.

I was in the Volkswagen Beetle fifteen minutes before we actually left. I sat quietly in the back seat with Karimot, Moruf and our family friends, the Sokoyas. I prayed that the car would not break down before we got to the television station. I didn't know or care what film we were being taken to watch. All I knew was that I was going to the cinema and I was planning to show off to my classmates when I got back to school. The usual twenty minute journey took more than one hour because there was a lot of traffic. There were some discussions between my mum and Mr Sokoya about going back home. I felt my prayers had been answered when we drove into the television station. We had driven a few yards when we were flagged down by a security guard.

'Good evening, madam.'

My mum replied, 'Good evening, we want to watch the film at the cinema.'

'*Mo sorry ma, bet ticket ti ton ma*.'

Hearing that the tickets had sold out was like a dagger through my chest'.

My mum confirmed what the man had just told us: '*Hah! Kosi mo rara rara*'.

The man confirmed that there was not a single ticket left: '*Oti ton pata pata*'.

I cried silently all the way home. Ironically, we arrived home within fifteen minutes.

Back in London, I knew I wanted to see the movie as soon as I saw the advert on television for *Three Little Ninjas*. Karimot and I discussed it and we agreed that she would ask dad for money and permission to go to the cinema. He gave her his permission two days after the request was made. I was ecstatic because my dream would soon become a reality.

The Friday night before my dream was due to be realized the cinema visit, one of Morufat's school friends Rita came to visit. I went into Morufat's bedroom to get something when Rita asked me how I was.

'I am fine. Aunty Morufat is taking us to the cinema tomorrow.'

'That's good.'

'What film are you going to watch?'

'We are going to watch *Three Little Ninjas.*'

'Oh, is it that film with those three karate boys?'

'Yes,' I said excitedly.

'You don't have to go the cinema to watch it, I have it on tape.'

With that statement, I felt I was within my rights to punch her squarely in the face. My whole world came crashing down around me. My dream was about to be crushed for a second time. Time stood still and it felt like I was falling into a bottomless abyss.

Luckily Morufat came to my rescue. She must have noticed the ashen look on my face.

'Don't worry,' she said. 'I want to take them, they have never been to the cinema before.'

I would be eternally grateful to her because she performed her big sister duty flawlessly. I left the room cursing Rita in my head.

I woke at 8am on the Saturday morning and was not surprised to see that Karimot was already awake. We did our chores thoroughly. I prepared my parent's customary Saturday morning tea and took it into their bedroom. When Morufat woke up, the first thing I asked was her was what time the film would begin. She said 4pm and so we would leave the house at 3pm. I didn't know where the cinema was, but I was scared that we would not be able to get there in one hour. I wanted to leave earlier, but I dared not argue with my older sister.

On the way to the cinema, I could tell by her face that Karimot was as excited as I was. When we got to the cinema, I leaned into the glass ticket as Morufat asked for three tickets to see *Three Little Ninjas*. I held my breath as the cashier tapped the keyboard and stared at the computer screen. She took an inappropriate amount of time and I feared I was about to experience the pain I suffered during my first visit to the cinema. I was convinced they had sold out of tickets and I was determined to lay the blame squarely on Morufat for not letting us leave the house on time.

'Would you like to sit at the front, middle or the rear?'

A sweet sense of relief flowed through my veins.

Morufat bought us pop corn and drinks. I had imagined that we would just go straight the screen, so I was a little annoyed when we had to queue while somebody checked the tickets. It was five minutes to four and I didn't want to miss a single second of the movie. I saw Morufat smiling at me because I kept leaning out of the line to check why the queue was moving so slowly. I was getting the same feeling I had a few months earlier when queuing to enter the aeroplane. When we entered the screening room, I stood still for a few minutes and stared at the giant screen to appreciate the splendour. I thought the film would start immediately and I got annoyed at every new advert that was shown. I was amazed when the place suddenly went silent as the lights were dimmed. I was transported to another universe for seventy to ninety minutes. I had watched many movies in my lifetime, but none could measure up to joy I got from being in that room for the first time.

The Interview

... I was totally unprepared for the journey I was about to take on that September morning in 1992. Over the summer, it had been decided that I would go the same secondary school as Morufat, St Augustine's Secondary School. I wanted to go the Quentin Kynaston School like Moruf, but I suspect this was ruled out because of the amount of fights he got into. Most of the fights he had always seemed to occur over arguments about food. I remember Moruf came home one day and told my dad that had been suspended for fighting. My dad asked him what happened. As he began to explain that a boy tried to force his way in front of him in the lunch queue, my dad burst out laughing. It had become such a regular occurrence that my brother was not even punished for getting suspended. If I had stayed in Nigeria, I would have had to have taken the Common Entrance exams in Abeokuta and would most likely have gone to Methodist Grammar school just like Morufat and Moruf. Based on the stories they told me, I am glad I didn't have to attend that school.

I was a ball of nerves for the entire week after my mum told me that I was going to be interviewed by the headmaster of the secondary school. While on the bus, my mum added to my anxiety by saying, 'make sure you sit up straight and speak up when the headmaster is talking to you'. We got off the bus and walked approximately ten minutes downhill until we saw the school.

It was five times the size of Christ Church. We entered the building and made our way to the reception area. My mum spoke to the receptionist.

'Hello, we are here to see Mr Morgan.'

'Can I have your name please?'

'My name is Mrs Kareem and my son's name is Kabir.'

'Okay, take a seat I will inform him of your arrival.'

We sat on a very low sofa and I took the opportunity to study my surroundings. There was a trophy cabinet with lot of trophies inside, an alternative entrance to the one we used, and some plants which sparsely decorated the gloomy reception area. I sat next to my mum petrified of doing poorly in the interview and disappointing her.

'Mrs Kareem?'

I looked up and saw a fragile-looking *oyinbo* man walking towards us with his right hand stretched out.

'Yes I am, Mrs Kareem.'

They shook hands and exchanged pleasantries. He then turned to me and said, 'Hello young man'. As I shook his hand and looked into his eye, I got the feeling that this was not man I would want to cross. He had deep frightening eyes and his voice made him sound as though he was a strict disciplinarian.

We followed him into his office which looked very basic. He and my mum spoke about me like I wasn't there. They discussed my previous education, when we arrived in London and home life. After a while, I zoned out and paid barely enough attention to nod and smile at the right times. Suddenly he looked at me and barked at me.

'What is six times eight?'

I was caught off guard but from his tone I knew he wanted as quick answer. My mind quickly went to the exercise book I used to use which had the time table printed on the back. In a split second, I responded.

'Forty-eight!'

'What's twelve times twelve!'

'One hundred and forty-four.'

'Okay, that's very good.'

I looked at my mum and she had a smile on her face which made me feel warm inside. At the end of the meeting, he walked us to the reception window and asked the receptionist to give my mum the required information regarding the uniform I have to buy. I had been accepted in St Augustine's Secondary School.

Induction Day

… I felt so excited as I put on the black trousers, white shirt and grey jumper. This was the first time I had worn a school uniform since Omolewa and I felt very dapper. My mum and I had gone to C&A the week before to buy my uniform. She bought me two pairs of trousers, three plain white shirts and two grey jumpers. When we got home, she told me that it was my responsibility to look after my uniform and to wash my shirts every day when I got home. She lit up with pride when the saw me and asked if I was excited. Inside I was petrified, but I smiled and said, 'yes mummy'.

I was too nervous to eat breakfast that day, but I sat at the table playing with the cornflakes when Morufat came in and asked, 'are you ready'? There was no turning back now. I was about to begin the first day of the rest of my life. I put on my jacket, picked up my brand new school bag, said goodbye to my mum and walked out of the front door.

As soon as the door closed behind Morufat, I was nearly overwhelmed with the desire to run back into the flat, grab my mother by the waist and beg her not to send me to school. The plan was for Morufat to take me to school for the first couple of days and then I would start going by myself. After waiting at the bus stop for five minutes, I asked Morufat what bus we were waiting for. She said, the 16, 16a or the 98. When the bus arrived, the journey seemed to take forever. As we finally got off at our bus stop, the area looked and felt alien to me. My legs felt heavy as we walked down the hill. Morufat must have sensed my discomfort because she put her arm around my shoulder and assured me everything was going to be alright. Her words of comfort were soothing until the school building came into sight. That was when reality dawned on me. My legs went in an instant from feeling like concrete to feeling like jelly instantly.

Although I had seen the school before, it seemed bigger and more imposing this time round. We walked up the stairs and walked through the double brown doors. I felt very insignificant and alone. The first few children I saw were wearing blazers and ties, and this made me feel very uneasy. We were directed towards the receptionist's office where we saw a number of nervous-looking kids with their parents. At the reception area, a black girl, who I later found out was volunteering for the day, asked for my name. As she flicked through her clipboard, I quivered with fear when I thought about the possibility of my name not being on the list.

'OK, here we are, Kabeer Kareem, you are in class Bede 7.'

Those words felt like a judge passing sentence for a crime I had committed.

'Go into the hall and sit on any chair in the second section from the stage.'

I was terrified about what I was about to face behind the oak double doors. I opened one of the doors and saw hundreds of kids wearing black blazers and blue ties with white stripes. I was nearly overwhelmed by an enormous sense of loneliness. I was hoping to blend in, but my incomplete uniform made me very conspicuous and vulnerable. I saw a group of kids looking at me and I was certain they would start pointing and laughing. I scanned the crowd and was shocked to see two very familiar faces who were waving at me. It was the twins Anthony and Andrew. A sense of relief washed over me. I said 'bye' to Morufat and eagerly entered the massive hall.

Anthony and Andrew both had broad smiles on their faces as I got near them. I felt like hugging them both but we touched fists instead.

'You are going to be going to this school too!' I said.

Andrew replied, 'Yesss! Levi and Cleo too.'

'That is wicked. That means there are five of us from Christ Church who go to this school.'

We all shook hands and bumped fists again excitedly.

'So what class are you in?' asked Anthony.

'I am in Bede 7,' I replied.

'So am I!' exclaimed Anthony.

'What class are you in Andrew?' I asked.

'They told me I am Aiden. I am meant to be sitting in that section.'

'What class are Cleo and Levi in?'

'I think Levi is in Columbus and Cleo is in the same class as me.'

As I settled down, I studied the twins, dressed immaculately with the full uniform, and I felt inferior sitting next to them. I noticed Anthony looking at me oddly and I felt the need to explain myself.

'My mum didn't have time to buy my jacket because she was travelling. She will buy it for me next week.'

'Oh OK.'

I settled down and I looked around me. I wondered if the other kids were as nervous as I was. I then saw a familiar face walk onto the stage; it was the headmaster who had interviewed me.

'Settle down, settle down.'

He was very softly spoken but his voice commanded a lot of respect. The hall fell silent immediately. He started by welcoming us to St Augustine's Church of England Secondary School. I was quite mesmerised by his speech in which he said that this was the beginning of a journey that should lead to great things for us all. I felt galvanised and truly believed that things would be different from Omolewa. His speech made me believe that I could succeed in this new school if I started working hard from day one. He spoke about the high levels of expectations he and the school expected from his pupils, namely hard work and respect.

His speech lasted for about five minutes then another man came on stage and introduced himself as Mr Richards, the vice principal. He was very different from Mr Morgan in looks and personality. He was a lot bigger, sported a beard and had a more down-to-earth and welcoming aura about him. I sat attentively as he said the next few days would be induction days for the new students. He then introduced the 'home room' tutors for the classes. Four people walked onto the stage.

'Bede 7, your tutor is Ms Mullen.'

The blonde *oyinbo* woman stepped out of line and waved at us. She was a lot younger than my primary school teacher and had a shy look about her.

After the introductions, the home room teacher for Aiden asked all the students in Aiden 7 to follow him. They all stood up and followed the teacher. As I watched them leave I felt a twinge of envy because their class looked cooler than mine.

'Could Bede 7 follow me please,' Miss Mullen said.

Like cattle being herded to the abattoir, we stood up quietly and made our way toward the hall exit. I felt lucky because I already had an ally in Anthony. It did not occur to me that some of the other kids might have also gone to the same primary school. I was a little surprised to see the other kids talking to each other as we followed Miss Mullen to the class room.

Entering the classroom fully confirmed that I was no longer in primary school. The classroom was bland and devoid of any personality. It looked like a science laboratory, there were six tables permanently bolted to the floor and positioned in rectangular shape, and one in the middle. As I followed Anthony towards the table at the corner of the classroom, I noticed that it had a chemical smell.

I sat on the high chair and started to study my new surroundings. The table's surface was rough and looked like it was made from oak tree.

'Settle down please, settle down. Hello, my name is Miss Mullen. I will be the home room teacher for Bede 7.'

I listened as she told us about the school, the plans for the day and the school's expectations.

At some point of her speech, I lost interest because I was looking around the class to see who I would most likely be friends with.

'You are likely to be together for the next five years,' she continued, which brought me back into focus.

I hadn't given any thought past the first day and now this woman was talking about plans for the next five years.

'Now I want each of you to stand up and introduce yourself to the rest of the class.'

I prayed that she would ask the process to start clockwise because it would give me a few more minutes to prepare than if she started anti-clockwise because I was on the second table and would have been the sixth person to say my name.

'We will start from this side.'

I let out a sigh of relief. When the introductions started, I didn't know that some of these strangers would go on to be my good friends for the next five years.

They first person to introduce himself was an *oyinbo* boy named Stuart. I quickly assessed and I concluded that I could take him in fight. Anytime a boy introduced himself, I assessed whether I could beat them in a fight or not. When a girl introduced herself, I assessed how pretty they were. Blacks seemed to be the dominant race in the class. I made an automatic judgement about a boy named Shawn. Although he was wearing the full school uniform, I concluded that he was a rough boy and immediately decided to stay away from him. The top button of his shirt was undone, the knot of his tie was halfway down his chest and he was wearing a thick gold chain. After he introduced himself, Miss Mullen told him that he would have to take off his chain because jewellery was against rules. He looked at her menacingly, and kissed his teeth as he took it off grudgingly. I could not help thinking that he would not dare try that if he was at Omolewa, he would have got the *koboko*.

As the introductions moved along the tables, I noticed that although everyone was of different shapes and sizes, they all looked similar because they were all wearing the full school uniform. I started to regret the process starting clockwise, I was not looking forward to the few seconds the focus would be on me. I did not know what the reaction would be because I didn't have a tie or blazer. I was scared Miss Mullen would reprimand in front of the whole class. Finally it was my table's turn, Anthony introduced himself then suddenly it was my turn. I felt the strain as all eyes were focused on me. I wandered what they were thinking and assumed they were thought I was not serious because of what I wearing. I instinctively wanted to stand up but remained seated.

'My name is Kabir Kareem.'

I heard sniggering from a corner and saw two black girls with their hands over their mouths and their bodies shaking like paint mixers. My pain multiplied when everybody looked at them and Miss Mullen motioned for them to shush. I was convinced that they were laughing because of my lack of full attire.

After the last kid introduced himself, Miss Mullen handed out a diary which she explained we would use to record our daily lessons, make notes about the homework we received and collect any commendations we received. She spoke for another fifteen minutes about the classes we had been assigned, and explained how to find the classrooms.

She then took on a tour of the school and I found the sheer size of the building intimidating. We took the stairs up to the third and fourth floors. She explained that the classes were empty today because it was induction day for us new students and school would resume for everyone else next week. During the tour, I felt I was beginning a brand new chapter in my life. I thought: 'Less than a year ago I was a skinny little boy in Omolewa Nursery and Primary School. Now I am starting my first day in secondary school in London'.

Baptême du feu

… My first few weeks at St Augustine's were like a baptism of fire. Nothing prepared me for what I was to face during that period. I distinctly remember my first Maths lesson which was delivered by Mr Aharas. He was Algerian with a big Afro and a thick moustache. From the moment I saw him, I could tell that he was a teacher who would not tolerate any sort of indiscipline. His opening speech confirmed my initial thoughts, but something else he said galvanised and petrified me at the same time.

'This is the beginning of the rest of your life. The hard work starts now. Don't tell yourself you will start the hard work in Year 9 or Year 10. If you don't begin now, I promise you will struggle when you reach Year 9 and 10. If you don't do well at the end of the five years most of you spend here, don't blame me. I have seen it before many times and it will happen again, I guarantee you.'

The speech brought home the reality that I was in a totally different environment from primary school with new rules and heightened expectations.

I had bought my tie and blazer in the first week and I felt so elegant the first time I wore my full attire. I was surprised at the difficulty I experienced when I first tried to put my tie on, I had always assumed it would be simple. I had to ask Anthony for help to put in on. While getting ready for school the next morning, I became frustrated after three failed attempts to put on my tie. I went into my parent's bedroom and saw my dad was sleeping. I didn't want to wake him up, but I also did not want to go to school without my tie on. I tapped him gently on the shoulder.

'Daddy, I don't know how to do my tie.'

He sat up and gently said, 'Right I am going to show you two ways to put on a tie: the Windsor Knot and the Half Windsor Knot'.

I watched intently as he slowly showed both methods and asked me which one I preferred. I chose the Windsor Knot method and that is how I have put on my ties ever since. Those few minutes are amongst the most poignant and memorable moments I have ever spent with my father.

The first day made me realise how small I was in stature. I had been a senior while at Omolewa and Christ Church. I was used to being part of the bigger and older group of students. The tables were now turned. I was a goldfish in a pool of sharks. Some of the older boys looked like giants. The classrooms were a sanctuary from the corridors which were uncharted territory. I heard so many comments about how small the Year 7's were and they kept referring to us a 'yutes'. I felt like a newborn antelope on the Serengeti being watched by seasoned predators.

Over the course of the week, I repeatedly heard the term 'battyman Morgan' whenever the headmaster was around. I had never heard this word before but I knew it was mean because they always laughed when they said it. I heard it again during lunch on my fourth day so I decided to ask Anthony about it.

'What is a batty man?'

He looked at me uncomfortably and spoke quietly.

'Batty man means a gay man.'

'What is a gay?'

I could feel the level of his discomfort rise as he mumbled his response.

'Er, gay is when two men have sex with each other.'

'What!'

He began to laugh at my reaction. This concept was incomprehensible and unnatural to me. It was impossible for men to have sex with each other, I thought, only men and women were supposed to have sex.

I felt lost a lot of the time because it seemed like everyone around me already knew what they were doing before I did. I had difficulty understanding what the teachers were saying even though they were white and English. Some of who had accents I had never heard before. On a few occasions I had to replay their words in my head before I could understand their instructions. By the time I deciphered it, I missed chunks of what we were being told.

During our first home room, Miss Mullen asked that we should say 'yes' or 'no' to school dinners when our names was called out on the register. The majority of people before me said 'yes' and very few said 'no'. I did not have a clue what she had been talking about. I assumed she was asking if we would be eating lunch on the school premises, but I also wondered if there was more to it than that.

When she called my name, I hesitated and mumbled 'yes'. She looked at me.

'Are you on income support?'

'Pardon?'

'Are you entitled to free school meals?'

I looked at her blankly and said, 'I don't know'.

'OK, does your mum work?'

'Yes, of course, my mum and dad both work.'

I will never forget the surprised looked that came across her face.

'OK, you don't get free school meals then.'

I have always wondered whether she was surprised by the fact that I lived my mother and father or that they both worked. I would not understand the concept of income support for another two years.

My classes were also very different to what I was used to and it took a little while for me to find my place. I had six different daily lessons, some which were completely new to me. In addition to the standard classes such as Maths, English and Science, I attended French, Music, Art and Design Education classes. Some were single periods which lasted forty-five minutes and others were double periods which lasted ninety minutes. I quickly realised during the first few classes that I was not the brightest in the class anymore.

During the first Maths lessons, Mr Aharas asked us to work out an equation and give the answer when we were ready. I was still copying the equation from the blackboard when an Indian girl provided the answer. I knew I had to step my game up. I understood most of that we were being taught, but Maths was never my favourite subject. I felt dumb because it seemed like other people understood the subject effortlessly.

I felt I excelled in History and English and was average in the other lessons such as Geography and Science.

Geography wasn't just about countries anymore, now we were learning about mountains, seas and precipitation. I thought Art was a waste of my time, but enjoyed Music and French because they were two subjects I had never been exposed to before. In our first PE lesson, I discovered that I was joint fourth fastest along with a Chinese boy and a girl named Shereen. I had fallen in love with her the moment I saw her on induction day, but she broke my heart almost immediately because she was one of the girls who laughed when I introduced myself. She was easily the prettiest girl in the whole of Year 7 but I felt that her attitude did not match her beauty.

I was on speaking terms with most of the boys by the end of the second week and knew the names of the majority of my classmates. Out of all the boys, I roughly guessed that I was the fifth or sixth strongest in the class. We all began to peel off into smaller groups according to our personalities. The black girls with the loudest voices were the most dominant group. They were always laughing at someone or complaining about something and were rude to some of the teachers. The Asian girls always sat together, and they were quiet, respectful and were considered the brainy group. The boys sat in larger groups, which seemed to form around those who played football and those who didn't. I always sat with Anthony but I spoke to most of the other boys.

An unofficial hierarchy was established with Anthony and Shawn vying for supremacy as the top dog of the class. I heard new words such as 'rasclat', 'bomberclat', 'jam-idiat' and 'feisty' just to name few. I didn't know what they meant when I first heard them but soon picked them up. The first classroom fight I saw was between two girls and the catalyst for the fight was the phrase 'your mother'. People began to schedule their fights after school and I saw brutal fights start with words such as:

'And what, what you gonna do'?

'Oi don't barge me, don't barge bruv'!

Other fights were instigated during arguments by a random person shouting 'ohhhh, are you gonna take that' or 'fight fight fight'. The people squaring off with each other would then begin to fight.

It was shock when I realised that after nine months of being in England there was still so much I didn't know. One day I was sitting on a table with Anthony and Shawn talking about which of the girls was the best-looking girl in the class. I said I liked Shereen, Anthony said 'Rosie is buff' and Shawn said 'that gyal Paula is thick, she got a big batty'. I wasn't sure who he was talking about.

'Is Paula the half-caste girl'? I asked.

The shocked look on both their faces made me feel like I had just committed a cardinal sin. Shawn spoke to me quietly.

'Kabeer, you can't say that.'

Confused, I said, 'What, half-caste?'

'Yeah, you can't say that, it's not allowed. You are supposed to say 'mixed race'.

I was confused, in Nigeria, we always referred to mixed race people as 'half-caste'. This would not be the last time I committed a *faux pas*.

Over the first couple of weeks, we started to work out who the coolest older boys were. It looked like there were two main groups. One of the groups was led by a boy named Mark. He was light-skinned, had big lips, wore a gold chain and always wore his baseball cap backwards. He always walked at a leisurely pace and knew a lot of the girls. His signature greeting was, 'yoosssh'. He became the hero of most of the black boys in Year 7, and we all tried to get him to notice us. It was the unwritten rule that if he said 'yoosssh' to you and bumped your fist, you were officially cool and was allowed to say 'yoosssh' to him too. Luckily for me, he took to Anthony. As part of Anthony's group he said 'yoossh' to me too and 'touched' regularly.

An unexpected but welcome surprise was the amount of beautiful girls there were. I had never seen so many groups of stunning beauties in one place in my life. Everywhere I turned there seemed to another girl more beautiful than the previous one. I would categorically say that one of my missions during my first three weeks was to get a hug from one of the Year 11 girls. The boys who got all the hugs were those who had brothers or cousins in the same year and I would look at them enviously.

Things were even worse when I had to watch from the sidelines as Anthony and Andrew played on their unidentical twin act to get hugs. One day during our second week, we were waiting to buy doughnuts during break time when we saw some of the girls they usually got hugs from. I had come to detest these encounters because none of the girls even looked at me. I would usually watch Anthony and Andrew with extreme jealousy and wanted to slap the grins off their faces. As usual they went over to the girls grinning.

'Where's my hug?' they said.

Again the girls exclaimed, 'I don't believe you two are twins, you look so different'.

I stood there feeling miserable when I heard someone else seemingly talking about me.

'Oh no, nobody is hugging this one.'

I looked left, then right. I was only certain she was talking about me when she walked towards me with both her hands stretched. I smiled and tensed up as she got closer and said, 'come here darling'. She put her hands around me and I got an instant erection as I felt her firm breast on my cheek. I hadn't enjoyed being that close to breasts since Mrs Kareem cut off my supply of natural milk nearly twelve years previously. The hug only lasted about twenty seconds but it was enough to make my day. I hung on to that feeling for many weeks after that. I knew it was a pity hug, but I didn't care, a hug is a hug.

Two incidents firmly confirmed that I was in a different playing field and I had to learn the new rules fast. A boy was running and fell to ground which caused coins to fall out of his pockets. Somebody yelled, 'Moneeeeey Droooooooppp!!!!!!!' Like vultures to a freshly abandoned carcass, people rushed to pick up the loose coins. The frenzy was over within a few seconds. I felt so sorry for the boy as he could only look on helplessly and dejected.

By my fourth week, I was still having some difficulty finding the classrooms in the school labyrinth. One day I got lost and was late for class. I came across two Year 10 boys having what seemed like a cordial discussion. All of the sudden, the one called big Anthony grabbed the other one by the back of the head and slammed his head into the glass door. I wanted to run but the shock rooted me to the spot. The boy whose head got smashed then smashed his own head through window causing it to smash completely. When I stopped running, I didn't know which floor I was on or which part of the building I was in.

By lunchtime, the rumour mill was awash with news about the fight. Most of the accounts were inaccurate and I felt I had to let people know what happened. I told Anthony exactly what happened and by the 5th period a number of people came to ask me what happened. During some of the discussions, I gleaned that Big Anthony and the other boy were the school's top resident hoodlums and were bitter enemies. I nearly wet myself when the deputy head of Year 7, Mr Aharas called me out of the class during 6th period. I had an idea why he wanted to see me. When I got outside classroom he told me that he had heard that I witnessed the incident earlier in the day. He asked me to tell him exactly what happened and said that I should not be afraid and that nobody would trouble me. Mr Aharas was an intimidating man and I was a little scared but I looked at him squarely in the eye said,

'No sir, I didn't see anything'.

'Are you sure?'

'Yes sir, I am sure, I didn't see anything'.

There was an awkward silence before he instructed me to return to class. As soon as I sat down in my seat, a boy name Robert who was Big Anthony's cousin spoke menacingly in my ear.

'Oi, Kabeer, did you grass'?

'Naaaa man, I ain't no grass'. I said nonchalantly.

'Ok, good good'.

This was my first unofficial test St Augustine's, and I passed with flying colours. I have always wondered what would have happened if I hadn't lied to Mr Aharas. Although I was still struggling to settle in and there was still so much I did not know, I had learnt enough within the four weeks to know that being a 'grass' was the quickest route to becoming a pariah.

My Pain

... I was going to school one Monday morning during my third week. As I neared the gates, I saw one of the boys in Aiden 7 lurking suspiciously. When I reached the gates, he approached me and said, 'hey Kabeer'. He presented his clenched fist for me to touch. I was a little surprised he knew my name but I touched anyway. I had seen him around, his older brother also attended the school and he regularly hung with the girls in Year 9 and 10.

I carried on walking and was even more surprised when he started to walk beside me. He must have sensed my unease.

'Don't worry bro. I just want to ask you some questions.'

'OK.'

'You are in Bede 7, aren't you?'

'Yes I am.'

'What's the name of that light-skinned girl in your class?'

I didn't know who he was talking about.

'You know, the light skinned gyal, big backside.'

'Oh Paula.'

'That's her name, yeah'?

'Yeah, her name is Paula.'

'Safe yeah, I will see you later.'

I felt the situation was peculiar but thought nothing more of it and carried with my business.

Later on that morning in Art class, I was talking to my friend Bashir when I suddenly heard Paula shouting.

'Kabeer, why did you tell that boy my name you fucking monkey?'

She looked furious and was shouting.

'Don't ever tell anyone my name again, you fucking monkey'.

I was stunned at this unexpected and unwarranted attack.

I was still trying to figure out what had just happened when I heard laughter from all four corners of the room. All eyes were on me, some laughing hard and others were giggling.

'What did I do'? I asked.

Tears started to roll down my face. This as was one of the most harrowing moments of my time at St Augustine's. Although the verbal assault was upsetting, it was the nature of the laughter which hurt the most. It was cruel and vindictive. I immediately deduced that there was an inside joke that had been bubbling under the surface, but Paula was the first to say what they had all been laughing about in private. The only reason I could think for being called a monkey was because I was from Africa. I had never been abused because of where I was from and it was painful. It was the first time I had been called a monkey, but it would not be the last. This was the beginning of a battle I would fight for a very long time. As I wiped the tears from my eyes, I saw that all the people who were laughing were black.

The fact that I was being mocked by people who I felt I had the most in common with made the whole experience even more painful. That was the moment I realised that racial abuse went beyond skin colour. It still hurts when I think about that incident.

Christ Church Elite

... My friends from Christ Church and I felt like we were an elite clique during our first few weeks at St Augustine's. Anthony was the de facto leader, Andrew was the lieutenant and Levi and I were the foot soldiers. Cleo was the eye candy of the group. For the first three weeks we went everywhere and did everything together. We felt special because we already knew each other previously. We were five deep and the biggest single group in Year 7.

We talked to other people during classes but during first break we would all meet, usually to follow the twins to buy doughnuts in the canteen. During lunch, Anthony and I would go and find the others then go to the canteen to eat lunch. After eating lunch, we would play hide and seek until it was time to go back to class. Sometimes Anthony would delay starting the game while he and his brother got hugs from the older girls. One day, Cleo failed to meet us at the usual spot for lunch. The next day, she failed to turn up for the first break and lunch. When it was my turn to do the seeking, I saw Cleo walking with a group of girls. She looked at me, smiled anxiously and waved. I waved back, but I felt sad and happy at the same time. I knew we had lost her. She looked happy and comfortable with her new group.

The rest of us continued with our routine, but thoughts of discontent and resentment slowly started to creep into my mind. I noticed that after lunch or break most of the boys in my class would talk what happened while playing football. I once suggested that we joined then and Anthony flatly said, 'no'. I was getting annoyed that we only did what he wanted to do and went where he wanted to go. Every time I went past my classmates playing football, I looked at them longingly but I didn't have the courage to leave my clan.

One day, about six weeks into the school term, it was my turn to do the seeking. I ran past my classroom friends playing football and I couldn't resist the lure. I stood on the parameter of the concrete pitch and I watched them. They were laughing and enjoying themselves like I used to do when we first arrived at the school. There was also something else which appealed to me: there was genuine camaraderie amongst them. I spoke to a boy named Tariq.

'Can I play?'

'OK,' he said, 'you can join Jeffery's team'.

Excitement and guilt jostled for position within me, this moment had a sense of inevitability about it.

The guilty feeling was crushed as soon as I got the first kick of the football. I didn't think about my clan for the rest of the afternoon. When class resumed in the home room before afternoon classes, the guilty feeling returned as soon as I saw Anthony.

'Where were you?' he asked.

'I was playing football.'

Our eyes locked and at the moment we both knew that it was the end of the Christ Church elite. I will never forget the hurt in my friend's eyes as he realised that his legion was slowly dissolving. After that day, we all gradually grew apart. We spoke occasionally but I realised that a friendship moulded on obligation could never last.

Politics and Respect

... In the first week of November 1992, Anthony got on the bus with me. I had been taking the bus by myself for about a month and I loved the independence. He saw me sitting at the back of the bus so he joined me. We talked for a few minutes then he picked up a newspaper that had been left on a seat. On the front page was the picture of President Clinton.

'Hey,' I said. 'He's just been elected president of the United States'.

Anthony looked at me confused.

'Is it, how do you know?'

I thought this was a very odd question, but I answered honestly with a bit of sarcasm.

'I watched it on the news.'

From the surprised look on his face, he probably found it strange that I watched the news. But I was surprised by how surprised he was.

Growing up in Nigeria, politics and the news was part of everyday life at home and at school. Watching the news usually meant family time in our house. When family friends visited us, it was almost guaranteed that politics would be one of the topics of discussion. The discussions usually revolved around about thieving politicians, bribery, corruption and even assassinations. The kids would listen attentively and regurgitate the information at school. There was always an unofficial competition amongst my friends about who heard the best news or rumours. Election times were the best. One of the most intriguing stories I heard was of politicians bribing people to vote for them by putting money in bread.

Back in London, a few stops before we were due to get off, a man sat in the seat in front of me and began to close the window I had opened a couple of minutes previously. When he finished, Anthony got up, opened the window and sat back down in his seat. The man looked annoyed and tried to close the window while looking at us sternly.

'Look guys,' he said. 'I am really cold, I need to close the window.'

Anthony stood up and stopped him winding the window up.

'My friend wants the window open.'

I was touched by his loyalty but also shocked at his lack of respect. I felt I had to intervene.

'It's OK Anthony, let him close it,' I said firmly.

At this point they were both grappling with the window handle.

'No, you want it open,' Anthony said, 'so it's gonna stay open'.

The situation was turning into an embarrassing farce. I stood up and physically removed Anthony's hands from the handle.

'The man is cold, the man is cold'.

My action seemed incomprehensible to him and his to me. For me, showing respect to your elders was one the most important attributes of being a Nigerian. It demonstrated that you came from a good home, a respectable family and had been taught excellent values. This was what compelled me to force Anthony to let the window stay open, he was a man and we were boys. Not carrying out his request would have been showing disrespect to my parent and the values they instilled in me. Although I been in England for nine months and seen kids telling adults to shut up, it still shocked me that my friend would behave is such disrespectable manner. These incidents exposed the differences in the cultures in which we had both been raised.

After everything had calmed down on the bus, I began to reflect. I remembered the first time I saw a child disrespect an adult in London. It was while I was at Christ Church and Thomas was getting told off by his mum in front of the school gates. He looked annoyed and said abruptly 'oh shut up mum'. I was stunned and was expecting her to smack him in his face. I was even more stunned when all she said was, 'don't you dare talk to me like that'.....

Thomas began to walk away and all she had to say was 'don't you dare walk away from me'. He ignored her and continued to walk away. I looked on astonished as Thomas's mother zipped up her jacket and walked away. I could not believe what I had just seen, although I had seen spoilt *oyinbo* kids in movies while I was in Nigeria, seeing it with my own two eyes felt unreal to me. I thought to myself, 'there is no way a Nigerian kid would even consider doing what Thomas had done'.

Being rude to an adult is bad enough but I felt telling your own mother to shut up was the worst thing a child could do. I concluded that Thomas lacked home training.

On the bus, Anthony kept on talking like as if everything was normal but I began to think deeply about how showing respect for your elders was a major part of my culture and upbringing. My day could not begin without me greeting my parents by prostrating and saying 'Good Morning mummy or daddy'. In the Yoruba culture, boys were expected to greet elders by prostrating and girls would kneel down. The Yoruba language also emphasised the requirements to show respects. If speaking to or referring to an older person, 'E' was used to denote their seniority. When speaking to a younger person, 'O' is used. Using 'O' when talking to or about an adult would be a major disrespect and was not fathomable for any self respecting individual. At home, I called my older sister 'Aunty Morufa' and my older brother 'Broda Moruf'. (Although Karimot just called me Kabir) I was expected to do anything they instructed me to do, refusal was not an option.

I sometimes felt that my older sister abused her position but I had been brought up to respect my elders so I had to do as I was told. I could not recall the amount of times Morufa would send me on errands to the shops while we lived in Akobo but I remembered one particular incident. I was watching one of my favourite programmes when she asked told me to go to shop to buy something she needed. I was angry and didn't want to do it but refusal was not an option, so I left the house walked to the top of the road. I waited there for approximately ten minutes before going back home and told her that the shop didn't have what she needed. I must have miscalculated my timings because she quickly deduced that I didn't go to the shop because I returned too quickly. She asked me if I really went the shop, I lied and said 'yes I did'. She didn't believe me because she put on her sandals and said that we would to the shop together and if she found out that I had lied, I would be in a world of trouble. I felt humiliated as I had to admit that I hadn't been to the shop. I was forced to go the shop to buy what she needed. My anger had reached boiling point by the time I returned home and my television programme had finished. Things changed a little bit when we arrived in London, although she still sent me on annoying little errands, she sometimes paid me to dry her hair with a blow-dryer.

While growing up in Nigeria, I read a text book which provided instructions about how to respect to elders. One of the most memorable things I remembered from the text book was that, if a child sees an older person sweeping the floor, he or she should take the broom from the older person and finish the job. Amongst other things, children should not interrupt an elder when they are speaking and should wait to be acknowledged, 'back talk' was not a concept that was conceivable, and adults could not be challenged even if you disagreed with them. Although our mother gave us a lot of leeway by allowing us to explain ourselves in certain situations, we never dare challenged any of her instructions.

On a number of occasions, while running errands for my parents in Akobo, I delayed my duties to assist an elderly person by carrying their load to their home or to the bus stop. They were always appreciative and when they asked who my parents were, I would tell them it was '*Alhaji Ele-fo*' and Alhaja Kareem'. I always felt proud because I had enhanced the reputation of my parents in the neighbourhood. When we arrived in England, I was always amazed and felt uneasy at how appreciative and surprised elderly people were when I voluntarily gave up my seat for them on the bus or tube. To me, it was not something I should be thanked for, I felt it was my duty. Back home, a child sitting down while an adult stands is a sign of ultimate disrespect. I had on many occasions seen my friends or cousins receive back handed slaps if they didn't give up their seats quickly enough for an adult.

As Anthony and I got off the bus in Kilburn, I made a vow to myself that I would never forget the values that had been instilled in me by my parents.

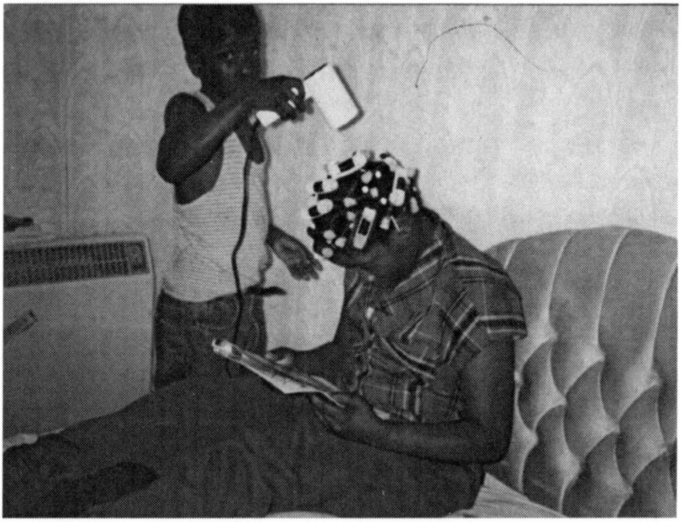

Working for the boss

Foe or Friend

... I didn't like the look of this boy as soon as he walked through the door. He had an air of arrogance about him that made me have an instant dislike to him. It was November 1992 and the second term had just began.

'Listen up everybody,' Miss Mullen said. 'We have a new student starting with us today and please make him feel welcome.'

'Hello, my name is James.'

There was no response from the rest of the class.

'Go and take a seat on the table in the corner.'

There was something about this boy I just did not like. As he walked towards his table our eyes met and it seemed the feeling was mutual. For the rest of the day his actions did not endear himself to the rest of the class. By the end of the day there was a general consensus that, as Rosie put it, 'he thinks he's too bad'.

The next day, during Maths class, I heard him speak to someone.

'In Africa, we don't use calculators. We do all calculations on paper.'

For a reason which eluded me at the time, I felt it was my duty to put this upstart in his place. (Looking back, I suspect that I was jealous. He exhibited the fact that he was African with pride and a little pomposity. Meanwhile I struggled to deal with the abuse I received because I was African).

'Well this is not Africa, this is London.'

'Shut up,' he said.

'No, you shut up.'

I felt I had won the first salvo because Anthony patted me on the back and Rosie said, 'go on Kabeer'.

During the first break, I saw him walking by himself and I thought that it was his own fault for not having anyone to talk to because of his attitude. We ignored each other for the rest of the day until we sat at the same table in the Science lesson in the last period. Things were cordial until he started to make comments to demonstrate his intelligence. He said he had learnt what the teacher was teaching us years ago in Ghana. He would periodically lean towards the person sitting beside him and boast.

'I learnt this a long time ago, all of you are behind. This is easy to me. Kids in Africa are ahead of everybody here.'

I became more and more infuriated with each statement and I could see that I wasn't the only one. We resumed our earlier verbal skirmish. He called me stupid and told me to shut up and mind my own business. I called him fat and told him that nobody liked him. The bickering continued until the teacher lost his patience and gave us both after school detentions.

If I disliked him before, I hated him now. I was seething with rage by the time the last bell rang at 3:30pm. The Indian teacher came to our desk and started to reprimand us for disrupting his lesson. We both stood up and tried to talk over one other while blaming the other for the disruption. At some point I called him fat, and he stopped looked at the teacher and turned to me.

'You see, sir? He is making fun of me again. I am gonna beat him up if he doesn't stop.'

I sensed victory because I found a weak spot so decided to go for the jugular.

'And what, you fat -'

I was not permitted to finish the insult. I was caught off guard as he lunged towards me with the full force of his body weight. I felt my head hit the wall as I tried to wrestle his hands away from my neck with no success. I was so surprised at the speed of the attack that I was totally off balance and fell over a stool. I felt him release his grip, I stood up quickly and tried to compose myself. My ego was hurting as much as my head.

As the teacher was leading James away, I heard him say, 'Sir, I warned him, he didn't listen to me'.

'You take your bag,' the teacher turned and said to me, 'and go home. I will deal with you tomorrow'.

I took and my bag and walked out of the classroom door. Six of my classmates were waiting outside.

'Did James beat you up, Kabeer?'

'What happened? Did you have a fight Kabeer?'

I started to feel overwhelmed by all the questions. I had just lost a fight, my ego was badly bruised and my head was starting to throb. Now everybody knew I had been beaten up. My eyes began to well up. I just wanted to go home but everywhere I turned in the narrow corridor there was someone who wanted to know what happened. Shawn pulled me on the arm.

'Kabeer, take him when he comes out, don't be a pussy, you can take him.'

I knew I couldn't take him even if I was prepared, but people wanted to see a fight. I was expected to stay and fight but I just wanted to go home.

On the bus ride home, I started to think about the repercussions of what had just happened. There was a possibility that I would be suspended for fighting, which would lead to me taking another beating at home from my dad. Everybody in my class will look at me as a weakling because I had been beaten up, and would call me a pussy because I didn't finish the fight. Worse still, the spot where I hit my head had started to protrude. But I decided to relax and deal with the consequences of the day's actions the next day.

'*Kilo she lori*?'

I was sitting in the living room watching TV when I suddenly felt three quick taps on the spot I had hit my head. My body went cold with fear when I heard my dad's voice. My first instinct was to lie about what had happened. I started to lie when he started shouting.

'Stand up when I am talking to you.'

I sprung to my feet immediately, faced him and put my hand submissively behind me.

'Eh, what happened to your head?'

'I had a fight with a boy called James.'

I was surprised I told the truth but I was too scared to formulate a credible lie.

'What happened?'

'He was abusing me in class. When the teacher was talking to us after school, he pushed me against the wall and I banged my head.'

I failed to mention that I called him fat.

'Who is this boy and where is he from?'

'His name is James M- and he is from Ghana.'

'Okay.'

With that, he left the living room and went back into his room, but I knew that it wasn't the end of the matter.

When I was getting ready for school the next morning, he called me to his bedroom and handed me a white envelope.

'Give this to your teacher when you get to school. Make sure you don't open it, right!'

'Yes daddy.'

I was hoping to figure out how I would deal with the one-sided fight I had the day before. I imagined the kids pointing and laughing at me as soon as I walked into the class room and whispering to each other, saying 'Kabeer got bust up'. Now my dad wanted to add to my misery. As soon as I got on the bus, I carefully opened the letter and started to read. I could not believe what I read. It basically stated that his son had been attacked and injured without provocation, and he expected stern action to taken against the perpetrator. I seriously considered throwing the letter out of the window but decided against it. I would have to deal with the consequences.

During the bus ride, I recalled two previous when my dad had intervened when he felt his children were being harassed. For the first incident, we were waiting to pick up Morufat outside her secondary school. She was unusually late and dad was getting frustrated.

'Excuse me sir, are you waiting Morufat Kareem?'

A nervous-looking boy was leaning by the passenger door window.

'Yes, yes, where is she?'

'Good afternoon sir, I am Morufat's classmate. She is currently under punishment, the teacher told her to go and stand in the sun.'

My dad shouted 'What?', got out of the car and slammed the door. He took in the air and seemed to inflate as he walked towards the school gates. Although I was watching him from behind I could tell his face must have looked like thunder because people hastily moved out of way. Just before he reached the gate, he bent down to pick up some stones and a small crowd gathered behind him. Twenty minutes later, I saw the crowd before I saw my dad and Morufat amongst them. My sister was crying and my dad looked the angriest I had seen him in a long while. The crowd had tripled in size but nobody dared get in his way. He was seething with rage as they entered the car and it had not fully subsided by the time we got home. At regular intervals he would angrily say, 'Nobody touches my children, nobody!' From the full debrief Morufat gave us, a teacher had singled her out for punishment because the whole class misbehaved. She was beaten and was forced to stand in the sun. The teacher went into hiding upon hearing my dad was on his way and the headmaster was left to try to pacify my father. That teacher did not return to teach at the school and the Kareem name became legendary at the Methodist Grammar School.

The second incident mirrored the situation I found myself in and happened when Moruf and I attended Omolewa. My brother had lost a fight with an older boy. When my dad found out he was livid and forced Moruf to go around the school to look for the boy. A small crowd had gathered and when they reached a group of boys, my dad asked him, 'which one slapped you?' Moruf pointed at one of the boys who was standing by the stairs. I saw their faces paralyse with fear as soon as they saw my dad.

'Which one, show him to me?'

Moruf touched the accused.

'*O ya fo lati.*'

I was stunned and I could see that Moruf was surprised because he looked confused.

'Are you deaf, I said slap him,' my dad repeated.

Moruf slapped the boy reluctantly.

'If you don't slap him properly, I will slap you.'

Moruf hit boy again across the face with a lot more force. I felt sorry for my brother because he looked weak. The other boy looked victorious because he took the beating with some gusto. I felt proud of my father because he had performed his duty by protecting his children.

I still hadn't decided what I was going to do with the letter by the time I got off the bus. I was surprised to see James waiting by the school gates as I approached. I decided to blank him and walk straight into the school. He approached me slowly.

'Kabeer, I want to say sorry about what happened yesterday.'

The arrogance had been replaced by humility. I could not believe I was speaking to the same person who gave me a swift beating the day before.

'I am new here and I don't want any trouble with anybody. We are both Africans, we shouldn't be fighting each other.'

I was perplexed and didn't know what to do.

'My dad gave me a letter to give to the teacher.'

I don't know why I told him about the letter or showed it to him when he asked to see it. He read it and started to laugh. His laugh was infectious and I started to laugh as well. He handed the letter back to me and said that I should give it Mr Hatch because in Africa we don't disrespect our parents. I didn't want to be, but I was immensely impressed with him. He seemed like a decent person and I felt guilty for insulting him. I was not to know that this was the beginning of a lifelong friendship. (Twenty years on, we still laugh when we tell people the story of how we met).

Are you a Muslim?

… The first person to ask me that question was a boy named Bashir that I had become good friends with.

'Yes,' I answered.

'Do you go to the mosque?'

'Yes, of course. In my country, dad used to take us to a big mosque every Friday, but since we came to England we have only gone to the mosque a few times.'

'Which one?'

'The big one in Regent's Park.'

'That's the one I go to as well. We went to pray there for Eid-Kabir some months ago. It was very different from the way we used to do it in my country.'

I explained to him that for Eid-Fitr my dad would buy a small goat to slaughter and for Eid Kabir, he bought a big ram. There would be no school and we would have a big party which would last from morning until night when all our Christian friends would come to celebrate with us.

The next occasion which I remember being asked that question was a few months later by two Somali girls.

'Why do you have an Arabic name, are you Muslim?'

'Yes, I am.'

I could tell by the looks on their faces that they didn't believe me.

'You are lying, where are you from?'

'Don't call me a liar! I am from Nigeria'

The one with the scarf said 'OK' sceptically. I thought that would be the end of the matter but a few minutes later they started again.

'Do you know how to pray and read the Quran?'

I felt insulted and started to become annoyed. I said 'yes' sharply.

'Prove it!' they said with a tone tinged with a sense of superiority.

I was determined to make them feel stupid. I began to recite

Al Fatia from the Quran:

> '*Bismillāhi r-rāhmāni r-rāhīm*
> *Al ḥamdu lillāhi rabbi l-'ālamīn, Ar raḥmḥāni r-raḥīm, Māliki yawmi d-dīn, Iyyāka na'budu wa iyyāka nasta'īn, Ihdinā ṣ-ṣirāṭ al-mustaqīm.*
> *Ṣirāṭ al-laḏīna an'amta 'alayhim ġayril maġḍūbi 'alayhim walāḍ ḍāllīn*
> *Amin*'

They looked absolutely stunned and I was vindicated. Sadly, this was not last time I had to prove my faith, it followed through my time at St Augustine's. I mainly got questioned by Arab or Asian kids. Over time I become angry when anybody asked me to prove I was a Muslim. I nearly got into fight with a boy named Omar because of this.

The question always infuriated me because my faith has been a constant part of my identity all my life. I hated the fact that I had to prove this part of me because I was a Black African. I believe there were two main reasons why I was so sensitive to this question. The first reason was that it always highlighted the fact that my name did not reflect my African origins or Yoruba heritage. Although I loved and was proud of the name Kabir because it translates into 'The Great/Magnificent' in Arabic, and is one of the 99 names of Allah, I was always conscious that it did not reflect my full identity. My surname Kareem, means 'Noble/Generous' in Arabic. I felt that my forename and surname reflected what or who I considered myself to be internally but was not representative of where I came from. My names represented a big part of who I was through my Islamic faith but not the other elements which made up Kabir Kareem. My middle name is Oladapo, which in Yoruba translates to 'Wealth mixed together'. I sometimes wondered if I would have had to prove my faith so many times if I had a Yoruba first name.

The second reason was that the question was another reminder of how much I had changed or was changing since I had left Nigeria. Back home, my parents took our religious studies very seriously from when we were very young. My siblings and I used to have Quranic studies twice a week after school. We didn't always enjoy the lessons and wanted them to be over as quickly as possible. It usually entailed us taking turns to read and memorise Surahs in the Quran in Arabic under the watchful eye of our teacher who would correct us if we mispronounced any of the Arabic words. He would nod off sometimes during our recitations and we used the opportunity to skip verses.

The long-term objectives of the lessons were for us to memorise every single Surah in the Holy Quran. My dad would threaten to send us to the Ile kewu (Quranic School) whenever he felt that we were not taking our studies seriously. He would lecture us about how lucky we were to be taught at home and tell us stories about how, when he was our age, he was sent to Ile kewu where the students received lashes for the slightest infringement. And we heard how he had memorised the Quran by the age of ten. My father got special dispensation for us to leave school an hour early every Friday so that we could go to the mosque for Jummah prayers. Friday was always my favourite day at Omolewa.

Every time someone in England asked me if I was a Muslim, it always made me a little shameful that I had not maintained my duties as a Muslim. It was another reminder of the inconsistency within me. Before we left Nigeria, I had memorised approximately 15-20 Surahs from the Quran. I stopped practising my recitations the longer we stayed in England and had become lax in performing my daily prayers. Over time I had begun to forget most of the Surahs I had memorised and only remembered four or five core verses. This served me well when I did say my daily prayers or went to the mosque, but at the back of my mind I always knew how much I had forgotten.

More than anything else, the question made me miss home, especially the post-Jummah ritual of buying fresh *boli* and *epa* (roast plantain and peanuts) or agbado sussuun (roasted corn) from the side of the road on the way back from the mosque. Without fail, our dad, my siblings and I would shout at the Hausa herdsmen 'eyin gan malu' (you yourself are the cattle) as we drove past them. They used to cause a lot of traffic when they drove their herds which could range from two to fifty from Bodija market on the main roads. This used to infuriate my father and would always laugh whenever he got an opportunity to abuse any of them.

It was the smallest things about home, like these incidents, that reminded me of what I had left behind: my favourite fruit, agbalumo, my grandmother's akan din din (fried crab), the general hustle and bustle of Ibadan but, above all, the sense of belonging. Sometimes I missed home so much, my heart ached.

Downfall of Men

… The first fight I had at St Augustine's was with a boy named Chris. The fight was over a chair in the science class. We went for the same seat at the same time by putting one butt cheek on the stool and trying to shoulder barge each other off. We were about the same size, but I pushed him off with relative ease. The ironic thing about the situation was that there were plenty of other seats in the room but I suspect we were both vying for supremacy. I was humble in my victory as I started to take my books out of my bag as if nothing had happened. But he was not gracious in defeat.

'You big nose monkey.'

This made my blood boil. 'What did you say?'

'I said you big nose monkey.'

I stood up sharply which caused the stool to fall to the floor and I lunged at him. I grabbed his neck and started to punch him in the face until four of our classmates pulled me of him. I picked up my chair and sat down.

By this time the tears had started to flow. I heard somebody whisper about me: 'He beat up Chris so why is he crying?' I hated fighting and this was the usual outcome of an unwanted confrontation. What hurt me the most was being called a monkey. This was the second time it had happened and I did not know how to deal with it verbally, so I resorted to the only alternative available to me, my fists, which always made me feel weak.

Our second fight was on the football pitch a few months later, again it was over something very trivial. We were playing football during lunch time when my friend Jeffery set me up to score. I was about to shoot when Chris ran in front of me, took the shot and scored. I was so angry.

'What are you doing?' I shouted. 'That was my ball.'

He mimicked me but in an African accent. He tried to run but I managed to grab him by his blazer collar and held him with both hands.

'What did you say?'

He grabbed me by my blazer collar and we both started to push each other.

'Let go.'

'No you let go.'

'It was my ball, why did you kick it?'

'It was a free ball, why shouldn't I have kicked?'

'Let me go?'

'No you let go first.'

We kept pushing each other until a small crowd began to form around us expecting to see a proper fight. The situation was escalating beyond our control. Although upset at the mimicking of my accent, I wasn't angry enough to fight him and I could see that he didn't want a fight either. I was about to take the high ground and release my grasp when the crowd began to chant: 'fight, fight, fight'. I then saw a group of black girls from Bede and Columbus running towards where the crowd had gathered. Leading the group was Shereen. I felt a sudden surge of adrenaline and testosterone pumping through me. A shocked look descended over Chris face as I tightened my grip and swung with all my might. He was totally unprepared for the escalation in aggression and I was able to throw him to the floor easily.

He got up quickly and came at me. I heard Shereen say, 'Go on Kabeer, beat him up'. Those words were a boost and I began swinging my fists. I landed two solid blows on his face, then held him by the left lapel of his blazer and swiped his feet from under him and he went down again. I felt unnatural doing this but I could not help myself.

As he lay on the floor, I stood over him triumphantly while trying to look as angry as possible. He stood up, picked up his glasses and walked away. I looked towards the girls hoping for kudos but they already began to walk away with the crowd. My triumph was short-lived and very hollow. As the adrenaline and testosterone began to wear off, they were immediately replaced with feelings of stupidity, guilt, shame and regret. Deep down I knew I was in the wrong but I convinced myself that my actions were just because he had made fun of me because I was African.

I continued to play football while Chris went and sat on the floor next to the fence. Every time I looked at him, the guilt and shame I felt grew. Although I had won the fight, he looked superior. The game stopped because a few of the boys were trying to coax him back into the game. The guilty burden forced me to go to Chris and say, 'I am sorry Chris'. He looked up at me and smiled. He then put his hand out, I grabbed it and held him up. We both re-joined the football game but I could not concentrate. I was still consumed by a feeling of guilt and shame. I was ashamed because I had always seen myself as a principled and righteous person and it was a shock that I had behaved like a bully. So to act like the people who had tormented me because I was African made me question who I really was inside. I also thought back to my battles with Bayo and George, and wondered if I was any different from them.

Commendations and Comeuppance

... I felt very proud when Miss Mullen gave me my twentieth commendation for cleaning the blackboard. While watching her sign the commendation section in my diary, I thought about the irony that I was being rewarded for completing a task which I was duty bound to do less than a year previously. I had been aiming for the twentieth commendations ever since the first student to reach the milestone were presented with certificates during the Year 7 weekly assembly a few weeks previously.

In addition to receiving my certificate during the next assembly, I had proof to show my dad that I was doing well in school. This was the primary catalyst for reaching the goal. I confirmed that my diary was in my bag before I got on the bus to go home and checked it twice during the journey home. My dad was sleeping when I got in and I had to restrain myself from blurting my news out as soon as he woke up. I decided that after dinner would be the best time to share my good news.

When the time came, I went into the living room and sat silently on the sofa for a few minutes. Without laying any sort of foundation, I came out with it.

'Daddy, I received my twentieth commendation at school today.'

He looked confused.

'Commendation? What is a commendation?'

'It is a reward teachers give to us when do things well. I will show you.'

I hurried to the bedroom to get my school diary, opened it to the commendations section on the last two pages and skipped back to the living room. I gave it to him and explained that every time a student did something well, the teacher would give a commendation.

'For every twenty that you get, they give you a certificate. I have got twenty and I will receive my certificate on Friday.'

He seemed to take a long time but I finally heard what I was waiting for.

'That's my boy, that's my boy, well done. I am proud of you. This is what I like to see, keep it up.'

'Yes daddy.'

Mission accomplished, I moved to take back the diary, but he was still looking at the commendations page intently. I stood patiently and waited for him to finish.

'What is this?'

He turned the diary to look at the front.

'It is my school diary. I use it to record any homework I get and a time table for my lessons.'

'Is this how you look after your schoolbook? Look, it is so dirty.'

I could not understand how a beautiful situation had become so dire within a minute. I now just wanted my diary back so that I could escape while the residue of his praise was still present. I had known my father for twelve years and I knew that this was not the end of the story. I watched helplessly as he opened the diary, shook his head and huffed.

'Your handwriting is absolutely terrible, woeful.'

A firm scowl had formed across his face. With each turn of the page, his face grew sterner and the disappointment in his voice was more palpable.

'*Oya, lo mu pen ati paper ko bere si practice ni sin sin yi.*'

I was totally dejected as I looked for pen and paper to begin my punishment of writing lines.

I walked back to the living slowly and sat at the dining room table. He gave me a textbook and told me to start copying from the first chapter. After copying half of the first chapter of the text book, I could not help feeling that this was comeuppance for a past misdeed I committed against my father.

My mind wandered back to particular incident the previous year which paralleled my current situation. While at Omolewa, our parents were required to sign students' exercise books to prove that they had seen our test results. The teacher would then check it first thing on Monday morning. Those students without their parent's signature on their books would get a beating, and would continue to get beaten and shamed until there was a signature. I hated showing my dad my exercise book because he would always moan about my handwriting or the mark I got for a test.

One week, I received an exceptionally poor mark in a Maths test. I knew that my weekend would be a combination of punishments, extra chores and not being allowed to play outside with my friends. I decided I would not to give my dad the exercise book to sign, but

I also knew that the lack of a signature would result in a beating on Monday morning. I decided that the only course of action was to forge my father's signature. I began to practice at my desk that very afternoon. I prayed for forgiveness during Jummah prayers that afternoon for the crime I was planning to commit. I practiced a few times on Saturday and I had it at near perfection by Sunday evening. Guilt weighed heavily on my shoulders as I stared at the awful result from my test. With adrenaline pumping blood through my veins I put my pen to paper and signed. I had set down a path from which I could not return.

On Monday morning, my teacher glanced at the signature, nodded and moved on to the next student. I watched with a feeling of sympathy and shame as three students were beaten for not getting their parent's signature. I became bold after that. I started to forge my dad's signature for every test. Three months after the first incident, I received a 70% pass mark in a Maths test. I was deliriously happy. I knew that my dad would be so proud of me. I wanted to tell him in the car on the way home, but he seemed to be in a bad mood. When we got home, he made sure that the housemaid had prepared our afternoon food and went back to the farm.

The perfect opportunity didn't present itself until Saturday afternoon. He had been on the farm all day and looked exhausted as he sat almost lifelessly on the sofa. I didn't care, I wanted my praise. With the exercise book in my hand I presented it to him.

'Daddy, I did a Maths test and I got 70%. You have to sign it.'

'Yeeah, that's my boy, that my boy.'

Second only to my mother's laughter, these three words were what brought me the most joy.

'Let me see.'

I handed him the exercise book. It felt like I was swimming in a pool of ecstasy.

'What is this?'

He was staring intently at the book so I went closer to answer his question. What I saw made my body and brain go into shock instantly. He had turned the pages backwards and was now looking at a previous test which I had failed. The level of my stupidity swiftly dawned on me. I was so eager for his approval that I had forgotten about the past tests I had failed and the forged signatures. I tried to buy some time and said 'what?'

'What is this, did I sign this?'

I could not fathom the depths of the trouble I would be in.

'Yes, you did.'

He looked baffled. 'I don't remember seeing this.'

He went back a few pages and he saw other forged signatures.

'This doesn't look like my signature.'

'Yes, you signed them.'

It took a lot a self-restraint for me not to start urinating on the spot I stood. I was fully committed to the lie and I had to see it through.

After a couple of minutes, he shook his head, closed the book and handed it back to me. I wanted to breathe a sigh of relief but held it in with the fear that it would expose my lies. As I turned to walk back to my bedroom, I realised he hadn't signed the test I asked him to sign. With brazen audacity, I handed him the pen and watched him sign. As I watched him put his signature by the result, I told myself that I was going to hell. Luckily for me, my mother returned from London the next day and my dad did not follow up on the incident.

Back in London, I wrote until my hand became sore. An hour after I started, he told me I could stop, but from now on I had to practice one hour of handwriting everyday and show it Morufa or himself. My only consolation was that I would be awarded my certificate on Friday morning. During the Year 7 assembly on Friday morning, Mr Aharas spoke for ten minutes about something I didn't really care about. I only paid attention when he spoke about awarding the certificates.

Students from Aiden were the first to receive their certificates. Everybody clapped as the names were read out and the recipients went to the centre of gym court to collect their certificates. My mouth became dry as the first students from Bede collected their certificates, then I heard my name. I stood up proudly and made way towards the collection point.

My joy was nearly shattered when I heard 'OO-OO-OOO-AAA-AAA-AAA' and giggling. I glanced at the direction from where the monkey noises was coming and was not surprised to see that it was being made by some of the black boys in Aiden and Columbus. I took a lot of comfort from Mr Aharas as he shook my hands sternly and said, 'well done'. I think he also heard the noises and wanted to ensure that my special moment was not spoilt. The noises were hurtful, but the certificate I held in my hand and Mr Aharas's support went a long way to relieve some of the pain.

Science Homework

… I eagerly wrote the deadline date in my diary and listened intently as Ms Mullen gave us instructions about what to do for our homework. It was a Thursday, and the homework was due the next Monday. It looked easy and I aimed to complete it to the highest possible standard. I planned to read it through as soon as I got home on Friday and complete it on Saturday morning so that I would have the rest the weekend to relax.

Up to the point of putting my key into the front door on Friday, I was still on track to read the homework as intended. While completing my chores, I realised that it was Friday, which meant that we were allowed to watch television past 6pm. I decided to start my reading at 6:30 after watching *Home and Away*. At 6:30, my motivation had decreased a little, and I reluctantly got up and went to get my school bag. As I walked past the kitchen, I caught the aroma of my mum's cooking. As soon as I saw *efo* cooking on the stove, I decided it would make more sense to start after dinner. When I went to bed around 9:30pm, my school bag lay untouched where I had dropped it when I got home at 4:30pm.

I woke up on Saturday feeling rejuvenated. I planned to make up for the previous days laziness. I intended to start the homework at 12pm and finish it by 3pm. I read the questions within five minutes and concluded that I would be able to complete the work within an hour. I was about to start when Moruf suggested we go and play football in the park. I closed my exercise book without any hesitation. We played football for about three hours and by the time we got home I was too tired to even think about doing the homework.

While eating dinner, my mum asked if I had done my homework. I said, 'yes mummy', with a straight face. I didn't see the point of getting told off for something I would do the next day. When I woke on Sunday morning I intended to make a start as soon as I finished watching *Little House on the* Prairie and *Rawhide*. After watching the shows, I washed my dad's work shirts and completed a few other chores.

Around 1pm, my mum told Karimot and I to get dressed because we were going to Hammersmith to see the Adeyemis. I ambitiously calculated that we would be back by 8pm which would give me a full hour to complete the homework before my bedtime at 9pm. I thoroughly enjoyed myself while in Hammersmith. I started to get a little worried around 6pm because my mum didn't look like she was about to leave anytime soon and I knew it would take more than an hour to get home.

The journey home was a nightmare. We left the Adeyemi's house around 6:30pm and waited at the bus top for thirty minutes. There was traffic on the way to the Hammersmith station and the tube train spent a minute too long at every stop. By the time we pulled into Edgware Road station, I was ready to sprint home. We arrived home around 9pm. I would usually be happy to have an extension to my bedtime but this was not one of those occasions. My mum shouted from the kitchen, 'have you ironed you school uniform?' I couldn't believe my rotten luck. I had totally forgotten about the Sunday night ritual of getting my clothes ready for the week. While ironing, I was determined to complete the homework while lying in bed before I fell asleep. Failure was not an option. While lying in bed, I took the homework out of my bag and started to read the first question.

'*Se eti ji? Ema late fu school o.*'

That was my mum's usual morning wake up call. I woke up on Monday morning and I realised I hadn't completed one question. I felt powerless and empty, because I knew it was my own fault and I hated myself. I knew the consequence for not completing my homework at Omolewa was a beating. Not knowing what punishment awaited me was worse than any of the beatings I had received.

During my morning prayers, I asked Allah to forgive me for all my sins and to get me out of the mess I had I put myself in. I was having the same feeling I did on that fateful morning I didn't wash my socks. My imagination tortured me all the way to school. I imagined everybody producing their fully completed homework and I would be exposed as a lazy boy. I would receive my first detention. Miss Mullen would send me to Mr Morgan's office who would in turn call my mother. I would not only get into trouble for not doing my homework but for also lying about it. I thought that the best way to avoid humiliation in front of my classmates would be to go and see Miss Mullen five minutes before class started and own up to my shame. My heart sank when I realised that the school assembly was on Monday mornings.

At school, after assembly, I hoped to talk to her on the way back to the class but I couldn't find her. When we got to the class, she wasn't there so I went to sit down at my desk. I kept an eye on the door while looking jealously at my friends laughing and joking amongst themselves.

When I saw Miss Mullen come into the room, I was itching to get it over and done with. Before she had settled down at her table I walked slowly over to her. I made a pledge to myself that no matter what happened I would not cry, but my nerves began to fail me as I got close to her desk. I had to tell her before the tears barrier broke.

'Miss, I didn't do my science homework.'

I thought I would receive some sympathy if I sounded remorseful enough. I hung my head in shame and stared at the floor, because I didn't want to see the disappointment in her eyes.

'Speak up Kabeer, I can't hear you,' she said.

I was forced to look up. The tears were about to start flowing.

'I didn't do my science homework, miss. I am sorry.'

'Don't worry, bring it tomorrow.'

'Pardon?'

'I said bring it tomorrow, now go and take your seat.'

Total confusion and relief consumed me as I walked back to my desk in a daze. Although I had been in England for nearly a year, the cultural difference still amazed me. Back in Nigeria, I would have received the koboko, been shamed in front of the whole class, or both. Instead of appreciating the reprieve, I became annoyed that I had gone through all that worry for nothing. I believe that was the moment my interest in my schoolwork began to wane which would go on to be one of my greatest regrets.

I'm from South of the Equator

... When we arrived in London on that momentous night on the 12th January 1992, I was wearing a shirt and jumper. It was cold but my adrenaline was pumping so much, I didn't really feel it. But it confirmed that I was no longer in Africa.

While staying in Hammersmith, although the heating was always on, I was still always cold. I hated going into the living room first thing in the morning because it felt like walking into a freezer. We slept with hot water bottles in our bed and a thick duvet cover every night. One morning I woke up and had to use the toilet, but it was occupied so my dad told me to use the one in the garden. I spent ten long and uncomfortable minutes in there and my only protection from the elements was a wooden door. I had never experience such discomfort while using the toilet before, my legs were exposed and the seat was freezing. After that experience, I either waited until the inside toilet became available or woke up before everybody else started to use it.

My mum bought us coats a few days after we arrived. Mine was blue with a hood, I felt warm when I wore it inside but was surprised I still felt the cold when I wore it outside. By April 1992, I felt I was getting used to the weather because I began to wear just a jumper to school. At the beginning of May, the sun began to make an appearance periodically. Between June and August, it was hot but not nearly as hot as the average sunny day in Nigeria. I was always amazed how *oyinbo* people sweated and changed colour because of it.

When I started at St Augustine's in September 1992, it had started to get a little colder again but it was still bearable. By the end of October I was having great difficulty dealing with the cold. It became so bad that while the other kids would rush out of class eagerly for first break, I would walk in the corridors by myself just to keep warm. On a number of occasions, I would be forced to go outside by teachers because staying inside during first break was against the rules. I sometimes pleaded with them to let me stay inside but my request was usually refused. I would also spend most of my lunch breaks inside the school building. I hated waiting for a bus if we went out to see family friends or going to school. I especially hated going to Vauxhall because the bus station was next to the River Thames, so the cold was always harsher.

We had a nightly routine in our house. At 7:30 every night, Morufat would boil the kettle and fill our hot water bottles. I first saw a hot water bottle at Hammersmith and didn't understand its purpose initially, but I could not go to sleep without it under my duvet by the winter of 92. At school, I was always found it amazing whenever I saw *oyinbo* kids just wearing their blazers. When I got dressed in the morning, my usual attire consisted of two pairs of socks, a tracksuit bottom below my school trousers, a thermal undershirt, my school shirt and jumper, a sleeveless puffer jacket and finally my coat. With all that on, I still could not handle the cold.

The second term started in November and my class were told that our PE lessons during the third and fourth periods would be off the school property. Initially I was very happy because I welcomed any opportunity not to be in the classroom and we would be playing rugby. I had heard the kids in Aiden 7 talking about it, but what made it so special was that Barnet FC footballers trained there.

It was a particularly cold Wednesday morning on my first visit to the training ground. As I got dressed, my mum came in our room and told Moruf and I to dress extra warm because the weather forecast said it was going to be below freezing that day. I didn't understand what she meant until I got outside; it was the coldest morning I had ever experienced. My survival instincts craved the warm bed I had just left, but I reluctantly and slowly made my way to the bus stop. It usually took five or ten minutes for the cold to penetrate my multiple layers of clothing but today my bones felt the full effects immediately.

My sole motivation for going to school that day was the PE lesson. I hardly paid attention during the lesson in period before first break. We had been instructed to meet by the coach at 11:15am, everybody was on the coach by 11:20 and we were on our way. There was a general excitement on the coach and I particularly welcomed the warm and cosy respite from the cold. The journey took about twenty minutes and I noticed that the further away travelled from Kilburn there was a gradual increase in the amount of detached houses and woods that we saw. I had never been to this part of London before; it looked gloomy and less populated than other parts.

When the coach pulled into the car park, I could hear the wind whistling ominously outside. It reminded me of the Sherlock Holmes book *The Hound of the Baskervilles* which I had read a few months earlier. There were miles of grassland with football goalposts on them and I could see a thick wood in the distance. I felt elements of the cold when the coach doors opened, but the odd mixture of warm and cold gave an indescribable feeling I will never forget. My initial elation disappeared the moment I stepped off the coach. The force of the cold shocked my body and my senses. What I felt earlier in the morning was nothing compared to what hit me at that particular moment. The speed of the wind on my face made me feel I had been slapped on both sides of my face and then punched for good measure. This cold was beyond freezing, it seemed cruel and unsympathetic.

The fear of stepping into the unknown flowed through me. I wanted to run back into the coach, but people were still coming out. My sense had deserted me, I was confused and didn't know what to do. I was relieved when I heard the PE teacher Mr Hatch yell at me.

'Kabeer, the changing room is over there, move it.'

I ran towards what I hoped would a warm sanctuary. I was disappointed when I saw a small dingy room which was just slightly less cold than outside. My teeth began to chatter as I reluctantly changed into my PE clothes.

A fog had descended within the space of ten minutes of me entering and exiting the changing room. I couldn't see the football pitches or the woods anymore. I paced in the car park as we waited for those who were still getting changed. I was tempted to ask the coach driver if I could wait inside the coach but didn't want to get into trouble. I put my hands into my tracksuit pockets to try to keep them warm. I felt unlucky and angry when Mr Hatch told me to carry the cones. As we followed him into the thick fog, I took some comfort when I saw the *oyinbo* people rubbing their hands together to try and keep them warm.

When we arrived at our designated field I could barely move as I placed the cones were Mr Hatch requested. By this point I was totally miserable: the field was muddy, my head was cold and I could not feel my ears. The students formed a semi-circle to listen to Mr Hatch's instructions.

'Right we are going to do some exercises to warm up?'

We did the usual star jumps stretches and drills but I did not feel warm at all. I felt the cold in parts of my body I didn't even know existed. He called us into a huddle after ten minutes and started to give instructions about how to hold and throw a rugby ball. I would usually be eager to learn new things but this time all I could think about was how the cold was damaging my body. For the first time since I arrived in England, I wished I was back in Nigeria. I began to appreciate the sun which I had taken for granted all those years. Even on the hottest day I could drink water to quench my thirst. There was no remedy to deal with this cold.

By the time teams were picked, my misery had reached its lowest ebb and I was starting to lose the feeling in my hands and legs. Holding the rugby ball with both hands became impossible because my hands were frozen and were involuntarily forming a clench. I tried hard to stay in the game but I could not handle the ferocity of the cold. A few of my friends saw that I was struggling and suggested I would warm up if I ran about more. I ran for a few minutes but it was so difficult I gave up after five minutes. I went to sit down where the equipment had been placed and watch everybody play the game. I pulled my jumper over my fingers and sat with my knees up to my chest, but my efforts were fruitless. I was close to tears when I saw everybody walking towards me and I thanked Allah that my misery would soon be coming to an end. By this time, I couldn't feel any of my fingers. I wanted to rush back to the changing room so I could run them under a hot tap but I could only move at a pace determined by this cruel enemy.

I was one of the last people to enter the changing rooms and went straight to a sink. I opened the hot water tap with some difficulty and put hands straight under steaming hot water. I did this for about ten seconds but it was not having the desired effect. Instead the tips of my fingers started to feel tingly. The tingly feeling gradually turned to immeasurable pain. I looked at fingers and was shocked to see they had turned red. I sat down on the bench and hoped that the pain would subside, but it just became worse with each second that passed. The type of pain was not something I had experienced before. I rubbed by hand together furiously but to no avail. I tried to hold it in, but I began to cry as the pain had become unbearable. It felt like somebody was torturing me by continuously putting pins in my fingers.

'Are you OK, Kabia?'

I looked up and it was Anthony standing over me.

'My fingers are hurting me,' I mumbled.

'Tariq, go and get Mr Hatch,' he said.

By the time Mr Hatch arrived, my tears had turned to full-blown sobbing. Everyone had gathered around me and Anthony was rubbing me on my back. Mr Hatch came into the changing room.

'What's wrong, Kabeer?'

'My hands are hurting.'

He took my hands and started rubbing them. His hands were twice the size of my mine, and my tears began to subside as the relief of warmth gradually returned to my fingers. In those distressing moments, I repeatedly cursed the day I arrived in this country and felt deep resentment towards my parents for bringing me here.

Revelation

... I didn't enjoy my Geography lessons during the second term of Year 2 at St Augustine's. Three of my main tormentors were in this class at the same time: Michael, Dorian, and Ozzie. On a normal day, I could deal with them individually, but for this lesson they hunted like a wolf pack and usually made it a miserable ninety minutes.

The last time I was humiliated by Dorian was two weeks previously during the Home Economics class when we had a cake baking assignment. When the teacher stepped out of the room, he said as loudly as possible: 'What you making Kabeer, a banana cake?' The laughter went on for about five minutes. At the beginning of this Geography lesson, the teacher Mr Calder stood in front of the class and rubbed his hands together.

'I have got a fun assignment for you lot. You are all going to individually develop a weather report and make a presentation in front of the class. What will make this fun is that your presentation will be recorded and put on a videotape.'

There was a collective murmur amongst the students, and I was a little excited.

'We will begin today, do the presentations next week and you should be able to see the video in a couple of weeks.'

He rubbed his hands together again and said, 'right, let's begin'.

He gave out a plastic sheet used on the overhead projector with a map of the UK printed on it and felt tip pens. He gave some instructions and left us to get on with it. The lesson was uneventful and I completed the task without being bothered by anybody.

I straddled between feelings of nervousness and confidence on the day we were due to record our weather forecasts. I had practiced my presentation in front of the mirror a few times and watched the BBC weatherman Michael Fish doing his reports. The reality of the event hit me when I saw a tripod with a large camcorder when I entered the classroom. When the class had settled, Mr Calder told us that each individual would have a maximum of two minutes to present their weather forecast. I was slightly relieved when he said the order of the presentations would be according to the register.

I anxiously watched the first few students making their presentations. Some of the other kids started to pull faces so to try to distract them, so to force them to laugh or make a mistake. After each student completed their presentation, my confidence levels dropped and the nervous feeling increased.

When I heard, 'Kabeer, you're next', all my practice and preparation disappeared as soon as I stood up. I was sure I would humiliate myself in front of the whole class and especially Shereen. As I stood up, I began to recite the Al Fatia under my breath. I put the plastic sheet on the overhead projector and stood on the spot where everybody else did and looked straight at the camera. As expected, some of my classmates stared to make faces. True to form, Michael and Dorian began to act like chimpanzees. The scratched their head with one hand, their armpits with the other and pulled the usual monkey faces. I was determined not to let them ruin my moment and I managed to block them out.

I began the presentation a bit shakily, but towards the middle I had composed myself and I felt I gave an articulate and accomplished performance. When I returned to my seat, some of the kids were still laughing and imitating an African accent. I also heard somebody singing 'hey hey we're the monkeys'. Although the taunts had become a regular occurrence, it still hurt but I did not react on that occasion.

Two weeks after we made the presentation, Mr Calder came into the class holding a video cassette.

'Look what I have here,' he said as he waved it above his head. 'Yes, you guessed it, it's the recordings from your weather reports, and we are going to watch them today'.

I had never seen or heard myself speak before and was quite eager see my presentation.

We all laughed when we saw the first couple of presentations but the laughter became sporadic as we saw more. My heart started to pound quickly as I watched the presentation of the person who went before me. The moment of truth was about to arrive and there was not escape. I smiled when I saw myself on the television screen, my first thought was that I wasn't very good-looking and wished I didn't look so awkward. Then I began to speak and I was flabbergasted by what I heard. I was speaking with an African accent! I went into shock. I always thought I spoke like everybody else, even better than most, but the realisation that I sounded like Nigerian newscasters and politicians made my head go into a spin. I was relieved when my segment ended.

It was approximately two minutes long but that tape had a life-changing effect on me. It was then that I had a crystallising moment. When the other kids imitated an African accent, I genuinely thought they were making fun of the fact that I was African rather than how I sounded. I went through the last thirty minutes of the lesson in a state of shock and tried to process what I had just witnessed. My mind flashed back to the induction day when the two black girls laughed when I introduced myself. I realised that they must have been laughing at the way I spoke and how I sounded rather than my lack of a full uniform.

I spent the whole lunchtime break in solitude and a deep reflective state. I became aware of myself like I had never done before and became scared that I didn't know myself as well as I thought. I became overwhelmed with self-doubt and a feeling of displacement. Questions began to race through my mind. Did I look like a monkey? How could I have not known I spoke this way? I began to think back to all the times I thought I sounded so eloquent and sophisticated, but I was sure I must have sounded like an ara oko (bush man).

Two particular events which had always baffled me suddenly became clear. The first event was in my English class in Year 7. We were all required to take turns to read passages in a book when selected by the teacher. I always enjoyed these sessions because it gave me chance to demonstrate what I felt were my excellent reading skills.

'Kabeer, can you continue from where Chris left off please?'. the teacher said.

'Yes, miss.'

After reading for about five minutes, everybody including the teacher suddenly started laughing when I said 'bugee'. I was stunned but not upset because I thought they all found what I said genuinely funny. Still smiling, the teacher corrected my pronunciation.

'It is pronounced 'budgie', Kabeer.'

This just made the whole situation more confusing. I pronounced it the exact same way she did I thought, so I didn't understand what everybody found so funny. I continued reading and didn't think anymore of it.

During the second incident, Michael came up to me while we waiting to collect our lunch.

'Kabeer, do you know the song from the burger advertisement?'

'Yes, I know it.'

'How does it go again?'

I was a little suspicious but I proceeded with my imitation: 'King-a-Burger, King-a-Burger, you got it'.

He laughed hysterically. I was happy because I thought that the exactness of my impression was making him laugh, but he must have been laughing at how it sounded in my African accent.

I was not able to concentrate during my afternoon classes. By this time, guilt became the prevalent emotion. I had never been ashamed of being an African, so I was having great difficulty trying to determine why I was so troubled by the revelation. I felt I was betraying my heritage, more importantly my parents. This was the beginning of a turbulent personal journey of self-discovery for me. Over a number of weeks, I became conscious of how I spoke. Whenever I answered a question in class, or read out loud in English class, I would accentuate certain words and sentences. I developed a minor stutter and began to find it difficult to get my words out like I wanted.

By 1995, I was into hip-hop music and Eddie Murphy was my hero. I loved everything about him: he was confident, funny and I wanted to be just like him. Approximately a year after the revelation, Mr Hatch said something which gave me food for thought. I had been in the changing room talking quite loudly to some of my friends while getting changed after a PE lesson. When I finished, I left the changing room when he casually called me into his office.

'Kabeer,' Mr Hatch said, 'I couldn't help but notice that you have developed a bit of an American accent.'

The statement shook me to my core but I tried to put a brave face on it.

'Well, after I finish secondary school here, my parents plan to send me to university in America, so I am just getting my practice in early.'

My reasoning was desperately hollow and I could tell that he thought so too because he nodded in a patronising manner.

I left the office feeling like a fraud. I could not understand why at nearly fifteen years of age I still didn't know who I was. A few weeks later I began to notice that

I had to repeat myself regularly because people didn't understand what I said the first time. I was so conscious of how I spoke that I would try to get everything out as quickly as possible. It was especially bad when I was nervous. My mouth could not keep pace with the signals my brain was sending. To add to my problems, I woke up one morning and my voice had changed. It became so deep that when I picked up the house phone, people thought I was my dad. My deep voice and the speed at which I spoke became so extreme that sometimes I didn't understand what I said myself, although I knew what I was trying to say. This became an issue at home because my parents could not understand what I was saying half the time. My dad didn't have a lot of patience at the best of times and he was not pleased when I began to talk the way I did. This has been a battle which I fought every day and continue to fight until the present day.

Resurgence

… One day, an *oyinbo* boy named Mark asked me, 'Kabeer, why do some Africans have scars all over their faces?'

'Because in some villages, to become a warrior, you have to fight lions and tigers.'

I expected him to laugh but he remained straight-faced and said, 'okay'. I felt foolish for perpetuating the stereotype. To remedy the situation, I called over to him.

'Oi Mark, I was only joking, they don't fight tigers or lions. They are tribal marks to recognize which tribe the person is from.'

I felt the only way I could ease my guilt was to give him a short history lesson.

'For example, before my country was colonised, there were hundreds of small tribes with different languages, cultures and religions. When the British came, they joined up all these small tribes and made my country. Do you know that there are over three hundred languages spoken in my country?'

'What tribe are you from?'

'I am Yoruba,' I said proudly.

He was about to ask another questions when the lunch time alarm sounded.

The conversation played on my mind for the rest of day, although I knew that the *Ila* were tribal marks, I still didn't know the basis for it. While my mum and I were watching TV that evening, I asked her why Yoruba people put tribal marks on their faces. With her usual serenity she explained.

'A long long time ago, there used to be tribal wars. The tribe that won would make the people of the losing tribe their slaves. They would then use the marks to identify and rescue members of their own tribe who had been captured during previous battles and turned into slaves.'

'Thank you, mummy,' I replied.

I felt a sense of pride at what she told me. I also realised that there was so much about my culture and tribal history that I did not know.

Between September 1995 and June 1996, I had gone through a process of self-discovery. A combination of incidents, events and newfound knowledge made put me on the path of defining my identity. I believe it began with that conversation with my mum, and was furthered by what happened in History class in September 1995. The teacher told the class that as part of the new curriculum, we would be learning about slavery for the rest of the term. History was one of the few classes I enjoyed, but I was a little anxious because I knew I would be the butt of some more jokes. We all listened attentively as she told us we would watch a film called *Roots* over the course of the term as well as using textbooks.

'We are going to watch a bit of the film for this lesson and will start with the textbooks next week.'

She put the video in the VHS and asked the person closest to the light switch to turn the light off. The class fell silent when the opening credits began to roll. Strangely my heart began to beat quickly. The opening credits were mesmerising, the drums made me think of home. I felt a little guilty because I couldn't remember the last time I had missed or thought about home.

The silence was briefly broken when the class giggled upon seeing a bare-chested women on the screen and the scene of the woman giving birth. I suddenly felt very special. Firstly because the film was set in Africa and secondly because the character Omoro was a Muslim. By the end of the lesson, I was feeling very good about myself. I felt an affinity to the main character, Kunta Kinte, because he epitomised everything good about being an African. He respected his parents, the village tribal elders and was proud of being an African. At the end of the lesson, one of my good friends Jeffery turned to me with a joking expression on his face.

'So Kabeer, did you live in huts as well?'

A few people laughed, which made a little upset and I felt I had to let them know that was not how I lived.

'No! I live in mansion with four bedrooms. We had a big compound in the front with small football pitch.'

I regretted my statement as soon I finished saying without fully understanding why. One minute I was feeling so proud to be African and yet I felt I had I had demonstrate to people that I was modern and civilised.

For the next few weeks, I looked forward to the History lessons. I had not been interested in learning about something in such a long time and I was eager to learn more about slavery. My emotions varied from anger, sadness, guilt and sorrow as I learned about how Africans were taken on ships to the USA and the Caribbean. I felt guilty when the teacher told us that the slaves that were transported were captured by their fellow Africans. I wondered if any of my ancestors had taken part in the capture and trading of their fellow countrymen. On other occasions when watching *Roots*, I felt blessed and superior for knowing where I came from. This feeling was most pronounced when watching the scenes when Kunta Kinte would tell his wife or daughter about his home back in Africa.

During one lesson, we were reading from a textbook which had a picture of a slave in chains. The picture was harrowing and everyone in the class gasped at the same time. Michael said, 'yo, that looks like Kabeer'. With this statement, I felt the balance of power shift. I was not angry or upset but I felt sorry for him. I found it ironic that he was mocking me, but he was the descendents of slave and I knew exactly where I came from. I saw a vulnerable side to him when he realised that he was laughing by himself.

Over the course of the term my confidence increased and I became thicker skinned. Although still extremely sensitive, I stopped responding to the taunts physically or verbally. This new way of thinking was put to a test during a Design and Technology lesson in February 1996. I didn't usually enjoy this lesson because it was attended by most of the boys who I didn't like and I hated the teacher. I had noticed that they didn't use me as their source of entertainment as much as they used to. During this particular lesson, I sat directly opposite a boy named Daniel. He had recently transferred from another school where rumour had it that he beat up a teacher which was why he was expelled. He was very tall and obviously very strong. In the first fifteen minutes of the lesson, I noticed him looking at me. For no reason whatsoever, he said, 'you are such monkey'. I was startled by the attack but I retained my composure. I looked at him and saw so much hate in his eyes. I had been in plenty of fights and arguments but nobody had ever looked at me like that before. I tried to ignore him but he kept on mocking me and then I snapped.

'Fuck you, you fucking bastard.'

I was ready for a fight although I knew that it would be a one-sided contest because he was much bigger and stronger than me.

'Shut up, you fucking monkey,' he said scornfully.

'No, you shut up, you big lip gorilla.'

I was surprised about what I said but the surprised looked on his face gave me strength because I knew I had hit a nerve.

'What? That doesn't even make any sense.'

'Well if I am a monkey, then you are a gorilla.'

'Look at you though, how can you call me a gorilla?'

'If you can call me a monkey, I can call you a gorilla.'

'Daniel and Kabeer!' the teacher shouted. 'Stop all that noise back there unless you want lunchtime detention.'

The teacher's warning put a swift end to our bickering. My heart was pumping fast; I was furious but felt very proud of myself. If I had been in the same situation the previous year, it would have ended with a fist fight and probably me in tears. I spent the rest of the lesson in a retrospective mode. Why did Daniel attack me like that? I had never crossed him but he spoke to me with such venom. I began to recall all the times I had been called monkey, gorilla or had my accent made fun of. 80% of the time it was by a West Indian person born in England who lived in a single parent household. I just could not understand why they hated me so much. I thought it couldn't be just because I was African. I began to think of all the possible reasons. Maybe my sensitive nature came across as weakness? Or maybe they were jealous because I knew where I came from?

James and I had become inseparable shortly after our fight, and we became best friends. James and I, along with a Columbian boy named Steven, went everywhere together. If all three of us weren't together, it was almost guaranteed the other two would be. It was a sad day when James told me that his mum was sending him back to Ghana to continue his education. On his last day, we shook hands and said goodbye like men, but I was so sad that I didn't know if I would see him again. I think it was a day in January 1996 when someone found came to find me on the football pitch.

'James is back, have you seen him?'

'No! Where is he?'

'He is by the reception.'

I immediately abandoned my position in goal and made my way to the reception office.

My heart was beating fast and I wanted to burst into a run. As I walked across the footbridge, I suddenly had a worrying thought: 'what if things have changed between us?' It had been nearly a year since I last saw him. I had made new friends and what if he doesn't get along with them? I became more nervous as I neared the end of footbridge. The first thing I noticed when I saw him was how much weight he had lost. He saw me and he broke into a wide smile. As we shook hands I realised that he was nervous as well. I greeted his mum by bowing my head slightly.

'Good afternoon ma.'

'Good afternoon my son, how are you?'

'I am fine, thank you, ma.'

'Are you happy to have your friend back?'

'Yes I am, ma.'

James and I talked for a few minutes before he went into the headmaster's office. By the time I got back to the football pitch, the news had spread and about fifteen people came to confirm with me that James had returned. We picked up right where we had left off. We caught the same train to and from school every day and spent every break and lunch time together. We sometime hung with different cliques because we had different lessons. I became a little jealous when he formed a strong friendship with a fellow Ghanaian boy named Kofi, but over time we formed an African clique. Being friends with Kofi made me appreciate growing up in Nigeria a lot more. He was Ghanian but he was born and raised in England and had never been back home.

He would listen attentively when James and I talked about growing up in Africa. We talked about, the sizes of the houses, the maids and drivers, the types of punishments we would receive at home and at school and the hardship that people faced which forced them to be resourceful. One day while the three of us were in science class, James was holding a pencil and asked if anybody had a sharpener. Kofi and I said 'no'. He thought about going to ask somebody on another table but changed his mind.

'Fuck it, I am just gonna do it like we do it in Africa.'

In one swift move, he bent down and started to sharpen his pencil on the concrete floor. Kofi and I looked at each other and burst out laughing so hard that the whole class looked at us. The *oyinbo* boy sitting with desk looked at us in bewilderment. I felt special being one of the select few who knew why James's action was so funny.

We talked about Africa so much that it began to get on people's nerves. One day, James and I were playing an African game when Micheal came over and asked what we were doing.

'It is an African game, you wouldn't understand it,' James said.

Michael rolled his eyes and said sarcastically, 'Woooo, it is African game is it? That means I can't play then?'

That was the moment I realised that he was using sarcasm to hide his hurt.

My last year at St Augustine's was probably my most enjoyable because it was the most uneventful. I been in the country for nearly five years, I knew the lingo and began the year on a more solid and equal footing. I was older, wiser and more confident than I had ever been. I missed home more than ever and that was when I became friends with a Ghanaian boy named Phillip. He had started at the school in Year 10 but I didn't get to know him very well until we sat together in science class in Year 11. One of the things I liked about him was that he always did his homework and would let James and I copy it before the lesson started. He had emigrated to England when he was fifteen and had an assured confidence about him. This sometimes made me wonder if things would have been easier for me if we had arrived in England when I was a bit older. I would be taking my GCSEs in approximately nine months and I was determined to buckle down so that I could pass my exams.

After the verbal sparring with Daniel, people began to show me more respect, maybe because I had stood up to one of the biggest boys in the school. A week after the incident, he and I became cordial to each other. Ironically, I had become relatively good friends with Dorian and Micheal. The more I got to know Michael, the more I realised that he was a very unhappy person. He was highly intelligent and funny, but I concluded that he lacked guidance. When he and I hung alone, I could see his vulnerable side, but as soon as he was in a crowd he would try to make them laugh by making fun of somebody. Every time I saw his 'bad' side I would remember a speech my dad used to tell me when we first arrived in England.

'You see these boys, some of them don't know who they are or where they come from. You should count yourself lucky that you know where you come from and have me around. Never, ever forget that you are an African.'

I didn't appreciate the value of that speech until my last year at St Augustine's.

Work Experience

... I was eagerly looking forward to my last year at St Augustine's because Year 11 students were required to do two weeks of work experience. Luckily James and I were assigned to work in the same place: Safeway's in Edgware Road. We were the only two in our year to be assigned to the same place. I found it funny that my first experience of work in would be the first supermarket I went to when I arrived in England.

I was so excited on my first day that I hardly slept the night before. To ensure I didn't arrive late for my first day, I left home in plenty of time which caused me to arrive an hour earlier than I was due to start. I was surprised to see James was already there. We were given our uniforms and assigned to different departments. I was told to work in the stockroom with an Indian man. I was a little disappointed about that because I was hoping to start work on the shop floor.

The Indian man gave me the relevant instructions and I began moving boxes from one end of the stockroom to another at 9am. After what felt like three hours of moving boxes, I began to feel a little tired so I asked my supervisor if I could go on lunch. He looked at his watch and began to laugh as he said, 'lunch? It's only 10:30'. I felt like weeping right there on the spot. He took pity on me and said I could go for a 15 minute tea break. I went up the staff canteen and bought a hot chocolate from the machine. The first thing I did was to look at the clock on the wall to confirm it was 10:30am.

As I sat drinking the hot chocolate I began to wonder when I became so soft. I could not believe I was so exhausted from just one and half hours of work. I began to remember all the times mum took us to Bodiga market in Nigeria. I would sit in the car and watch pityingly as *alaru* (load carriers) kids who were usually my age or sometimes younger carrying loads which was ten times their own body weight. A donkey would have struggled to carry some of the load they carried. I once witnessed an incident on one our trips to the market which had a lasting effect on me. Karimot and I were waiting in the car when I saw an *alaru* that looked just like my little sister; she seemed about eight or nine years- old. She was following a woman and I watched as she struggled to balance the woman's heavy load on her head. When they got to the car, she loaded the woman's car then waited patiently. What I saw next was the cruellest thing I had ever seen, as the woman drove off without paying the girl. The girl feebly ran after the car shouting, '*mummy e jowo, e jowo*' (mummy please, please). She stopped running and watched dejected as the car drove off in the distance. Then she turned around and went to look for more loads to carry. I wanted to cry for her.

Remembering this incident at Safeways made feel ashamed of myself. Those kids didn't have childhoods and got paid a pittance for doing the hardest job in world. Here I was feeling the strain after working for less than two hours. I decided to go back downstairs five minutes before I was due to return and worked until I was told to go to lunch. My first day was exhausting but the memory of the dejected look on that little girl's face kept me going for the rest of the day. When I got home that evening, I was shattered but I was proud that I made it through the day.

Things became easier over the next two days. James and I didn't get to work together much, which was probably for the best because we would have talked non-stop. We worked in different departments over the course of the week. I enjoyed working in the produce section but hated the chilled section. On my fourth day, my supervisor asked me to help with the packing at the tills. I had packed about ten customers' shopping when one of them asked if I would mind taking the shopping to her car. I agreed and waited for her by the exit while she completed her payments. I followed her to her car which was about two minutes from the store and loaded her shopping into the boot. When I finished she said, 'thank you' and gave me £2. I was very surprised and wanted to reject it but I took and said, 'thank you madam'.

When I returned to the store, I saw James packing bags at the till and whispered to him that I just go a tip. During our afternoon break that day, we got talking to one of staff who told us that on a good day, he could make £50 in tips. The next day James and I began to finish our work on the shop floor quickly so that we would be assigned to the tills. I made £8 in tips. We did not work over the weekend, but I was eager to get back to work on Monday morning. We soon realised that the customers we got had a lot to do with luck, some tipped and others didn't. We began to take it in our stride. The journeys also varied from taking the shopping to their cars or to their houses and we tried to guess the size of the tip by the car or where they lived.

On the Monday, I was packing at the till at 5:30 pm when a posh *oyinbo* woman asked if I could take her bags home for her. I was due to finish at 6pm but she looked rich so I thought she would tip well. Her apartment was over twenty minutes away from the store. I thought I had hit the jackpot when a doorman opened the doors for her when she entered a building which was obviously for the rich. I took the shopping into her kitchen hoping that she would be impressed with the extra effort. After I finished, I slowly walked to the front door. This was usually the stage where I would receive my tip. I stepped out of the front door and was shocked when I heard 'thank you' and the door slam shut behind me. Although on a very different scale, I understood how the little girl felt as she watched the car drive away. I didn't get back to store till 6:30 and was cursing the woman all the way. I was very touched when I found James waiting for me.

The next day, I felt I had drawn the short straw when a black family with a mountain of shopping came to use the till which I was packing. It was ten minutes before my lunch and I was hungry and didn't want to want push a trolley anywhere. I asked if they wanted home service. The only consolation I took when they accepted my offer was that they had spent over £100 so I may get a tip. On the way to their house, I heard them speaking Yoruba and realised that they had emigrated from Nigeria and recently arrived in London. I could not help but think about when we first arrived five years earlier. The hunger and nostalgia must have made me lose concentration because the wheels of the trolley hit a raised part of the pavement which caused some the goods to fall off. My first thought when the bags hit the floor was, 'shit, there goes my tip'. I felt bad when I saw that I had broken their eggs. I apologised repeatedly and the girl said, 'don't worry it's ok'. When we got to their apartment, we all unloaded the shopping and as I left I said 'sorry' one more time. I heard the dad say, 'young man, wait'. I was sure he was going to tell me off for breaking the eggs but I was stunned when I turned to see the girl holding a £10 note. I felt so guilty that I refused, but that the dad insisted so I took it. I prostrated and said '*e se sir*' (thank you, sir).

On the second to last day of working in the store, I was working in the produce section when the store manager called me over to him.

'I need you to help the president.'

'Pardon? Which president?'

'President Mugabe, he shops here when he is in the country.'

I went weak in the knees, I was not a fan or an admirer of his but this was the head of state of an African country. James and I were told to get trolleys and follow him around the store. After getting the trolleys, we waited by entrance and watched excitedly as a convoy of three Mercedes Benzes with Zimbabwe flags on them pulled up outside the store. Six burly black men jumped out of the car and one of them opened the door of the Mercedes in the middle. When I first saw him, my first thought was that he looked so small. When he reached us, he looked at us and said hello. I was so nervous I didn't know whether to say 'hello' or salute. James and I both responded with 'good afternoon, sir'.

We followed him around the store for about two hours. He would point to what he wanted and one of the bodyguards would pick it and put it in the trolley. I didn't know much about him, but I knew that all Africans leaders were rich. I was certain that we would receive the biggest tip ever, at least £50 each minimum. After packing his goods and loading it in the car, one of the bodyguards gave James £20. It was £30 less than what I was expecting but it would be my biggest tip so far. I astonished when he said, 'for both of you.

A Mother's Love

.... My last teacher/parents evening session at St Augustine's was one of the most significant and life changing event of my life. It was a few months after my work experience at Safeway's and the objective of the evening was to discuss the student's preparation for the GCSE exams and beyond. I was not performing as well as I should have been at school and I knew my mum would be disappointed in me. The first three teachers we saw said the same things, 'Kabir is bright young man, but just fails to apply him' 'He is very intelligent but lacks concentration'.

The 4th teacher that we saw was my science teacher, an oyinbo man named Mr Oakley. He basically told my mum that I was a poor student, and as a result of my poor academic record I would only be allowed to sit the lower tier GCSE exam. The highest grade I could get was a C and he didn't even think I achieve this grade. I went into my own little world as he and my mum talked about me and what my options were, I watched as this man made me feel like I was a lost cause and had no hope. Then I heard the statement which would which would change my life forever, 'Frankly he is not University Material. He would probably be better in a profession like carpentry or using his hand'.

The depths of the feelings of worthlessness which I felt at that moment are immeasurable. I had my doubts about whether I could make it to university but to hear a teacher confirm it made me feel that my all parent's sacrifices had all been for nothing. Then I heard, 'How dare you say that? I looked at my mum and she looked the angriest I had ever seen her in my life.

'It's my professional opinion as his science teacher Mrs Kareem', said Mr Oakley.

'What gives you the right to say that', my mum said. You are his teacher, you are supposed to by encouraging and supporting him not putting him down. Is this how you treat all your students? What kind of teacher are you'? `I believe that my son can achieve anything he puts his mind to`.

Mr Oakley went as red as a lobster as my mum continued her rebuke. He tried to explain himself but all that came out were mumbles. He apologised to my mum for upsetting her and after a few more minutes of talking about my exam options for my forthcoming exams, we got up to leave. As we left the desk, my mum called him an idiot.

I was initially angry at myself for putting my mother in such a position and then I became petrified that I would not be able to fulfil the immense belief that she obviously saw in me. I did not have the same level of confidence she had in my abilities and I was afraid I would let her down. At that moment, I did not realise that the belief my mum showed in me that evening would be the greatest single inspiration in my life. It was the driving force behind some of my greatest accomplishments and gave me the strength to deal with many difficult moments in my life. (The value of the belief my mother has shown in me that evening was most significant on the 17th of June 2003 when I was awarded my Bachelor of Arts with Honours Degree in Business and Marketing from Middlesex University).

Epilogue

The school bell rang at 3.30pm and it sent shivers down my spine; it had exposed the conclusiveness of that chapter of my life. I believe that was the moment I made the complete transition from childhood/adolescence to manhood. I began the journey down memory lane as a child but had become a man by the time I finished. Those couple of hours on the bench turned out to be the hinge between my childhood and adulthood and I will never forget it.

A quote by Ralph Waldo Emerson – "Life is a journey, not the destination" – embodied how I felt that afternoon. I had always thought that the most significant day of my life was January 12 1992 when I made the journey to London. But I realised it was the 'moments' in my life which had defined who I was and who I would turn out to be. It had been a journey of self-discovery which took me further back into my childhood than I had anticipated. The fulfilment I got from conjuring up memories that had lain dormant for years is immeasurable and I was truly appreciative. I felt very lucky to have been able to experience two very different cultures during my formative years. This had given my life richness and adventure that few people could ever experience and I would be grateful to my parents for this forever.

The fear and anxiety which I had been feeling for the previous few weeks and up till the point I sat on the bench had begun to recede. I became confident and decided that instead of fearing the change I would embrace it. I had faced one of the biggest challenges of my life when I left my home and all I had known as a naïve and excited 11 year old boy. 'My TRANSITION' was very emotional and difficult at times but as a result, I had experienced some of the most memorable moments in my lifetime. I was amazed at how quickly I had matured and how I continuously adapted to my ever-changing environment.

I had not missed Nigeria so much at any point since I left much as I did that afternoon, yet I had never felt more at home in England either. I missed the vibrancy and constant energy of my motherland, but I appreciated the hours of tranquillity I spent in London parks. I missed the opportunity of sitting on the veranda with my siblings during a blackout, but also appreciated the straight forward life I had become accustomed to. I missed my favourite fruits, my family and my community. The list of the things I missed about Nigeria was endless, but the thing I missed the most was fresh *boli* and *epa*.

One of the most significant things I realised about myself that afternoon was that the biggest struggle I faced in my short 16 years was within myself. I was a very sensitive person which I originally saw as a weakness but came to realise could be one of my greatest strengths. I regretted not having more self-belief and giving up so easily at crucial times. Then I thought about all the challenges I had overcome, the cultural differences – adapting to the weather took the best part of three years.

I had taught myself to swim again, I had shared laughter with people (some of whom were sat on the bench with me) who had brought tears to my eyes, and I was finally happy with who I was. I thought about how significant my identity was to me and all the different elements that made up Kabir Kareem. My origin is African; I am of dual citizenship, Nigerian and British; my race is Black, my faith is Islam, my tribe is Yoruba, my ethnicity is Egba, and I am a descendant of the clan city of Abeokuta, the town of Ijaye and the village of Igbore. I had finally found myself.

While saying goodbye to my friends, I thought about what my life would have been like if I hadn't left Nigeria; I wondered when I would go back and how much of what I remembered would have changed. I wondered if my childhood friends in Akobo would remember me and how far they had moved on with their lives. I hoped to find out soon. As I walked out of the school gates for the last time as a student, I felt a lot more prepared and confident than when I had entered five years previously.

I went back to St Augustine's over the next couple of weeks to complete my GCSE exams. During that period I began to make plans to get a job over the summer. It would be my first step towards independence and I could not wait to start earning my own money. I eagerly looked forward to what I considered to be the next chapter of my life. I felt the world was my oyster; I was in charge of my own destiny and was prepared to deal with any challenges that came my way.

As soon as I finished my last exam, I went to the hotel near St Augustine's to ask if they had any job vacancies. I was hoping they had a vacancy for a porter or something similar. I was disappointed but not disheartened when the receptionist said that there were no vacancies. I went home and made a plan to go to Oxford Circus the next day and go into every shop to ask if they had vacancies. When I told Morufat my plan, she suggested that I should go and register at the local job centre because I would stand a better chance of getting a job.

When I woke the next morning I went to the job centre and registered. I applied for approximately ten jobs ranging from customer service assistants at the local supermarkets to a crew member at McDonald's. I went to Oxford Circus in the afternoon and went to the clothing store C&A to ask if there were any vacancies. I was so happy when one of the store clerks handed me an application form to complete. I completed it as fully as possible and proudly set out my duties during my two weeks' work experience at Safeway's. I felt I had done enough for the day so I went home.

I was ecstatic when I received three letters inviting me to interviews the following week. One was from C&A, another was for Sainsbury's supermarket and the third was for Safeway's supermarket. I could not believe how easy it was. I attended all the interviews over the course of three days the following week. I left each interview convinced that it went brilliantly because I had put myself across excellently. When I got home after the third interview, I walked into the kitchen where my mum was cooking and she asked me how it went.

'It went very well, I said.

'That's good.'

'Mummy, how will I decide which job to take?'

I began to go through the pros and cons of each role and decided that I would accept the Sainsbury's job when it was offered to me. As I was speaking, my mum had a strange look on her face. She was nodding in a supportive manner but something about the look on her face just didn't feel right but I could not decipher what it was.

Sainsbury's was the job I wanted the most and C&A was my second choice. I didn't even consider the Safeway's job because it was not appealing at all because they paid the least and I didn't particularly like the interviewer. I faced a conundrum because I attended the C&A interview first and the Sainsbury's interview second, so I expected to hear back from C&A first.

'Mummy, you know what, when C&A give me the job should I accept and then tell them I don't want it when I get the Sainsbury's job?

'It's up to you.'

The longer we spoke, the more pensive she looked. She was nodding and smiling at me encouragingly but was looking at me intently like she was struggling to holding something back. I decided that out of principle I would not accept the C&A job but accept the Sainsbury's job instead.

I eagerly checked the post every day the following week and was disappointed when I didn't see any letters for me. I didn't bother going to the job centre or to apply for any other jobs during this period. Approximately a week after my first interview, Karimot handed me a letter which had a C&A logo on it. I slowly opened the envelope and began to read the letter. I was a little disappointed because it wasn't from Sainsbury's.

I read the first few lines: 'Thank you for attending the interview at...'

The next paragraph started with 'Unfortunately we cannot offer you a position at this time...'

I felt insulted; I believed it was an easy job that anybody could do and was perplexed as to why I didn't get it. It was a customer services job which mainly consisted of tidying and folding clothes. I felt I could do it in my sleep. I read the rest of the letter which gave the reason as lack of experience. I put the letter away nonchalantly and carried on watching television. When my mum returned from work that evening, she asked if I had heard anything.

'I didn't get the job at C&A,' I said.

'Oh, I'm sorry.'

I shrugged my shoulders and said, 'I didn't want that job anyway.'

A couple of days after the rejection letter from C&A, I eagerly opened a letter from Sainsbury's. This was the job I wanted and as I opened the letter I began to imagine what I would buy with my first pay. I had opened my own bank account in the anticipation of getting paid at least £150 pounds a week. The letter started much like the previous one, thanking me for attending the interview. I was flabbergasted when I read the beginning of the next paragraph:

Unfortunately we will not be processing your application to the next stage of the recruitment process.'

I read the sentence three times to make sure that what I read was correct and checked the logo on the letter to confirm it was really from Sainsbury's. It took a few minutes for it to sink in. I suddenly became exhausted as I walked up the stairs to my bedroom. I lay on my bed and reviewed the interview in my head trying to pin point where it could have gone wrong. I felt I had spoken with confidence; I had emphasised my two weeks' work experience at Safeway's, and the team working skill developed to earn my Duke of Edinburgh Bronze award.

I was so sure that I had got the job because of the rapport I had with the interviewer; she was so nice and friendly and nodded intently as I gave my answers. She made me feel like I was perfect for the job and I was sure the job was mine when I left the interview. As she walked me to the exit door, I laughed and joked with her and told her about my school trip to Paris. We shook hands firmly and she said with a broad smile 'I hope to see you soon'. I could not understand what could have gone wrong. I lay in my bed feeling sorry for myself for about an hour.

I left the bedroom feeling dejected that I didn't get my first or second choices and would have to settle for the third option. I was certain I had got the job at Safeway's. It was a large recruitment drive and the interviewer had told me that there were a number of positions available in various departments within the store. In addition, I had experience of working at the company. It was less money than the other companies and the store was not as glamorous. I decided I would take the job, gain some experience and go for a bigger, better job later in the summer.

The next day, I woke and went straight to the post box to check if I had any letters. There was only one letter and it was for me. I felt like the world owed me something and I deserved better. I grudgingly opened the letter and went straight to the second paragraph. My legs nearly gave way as I read:

'Unfortunately we will not...'

I wanted to start crying right there on the spot. I instantly became disorientated and I had to lean on the wall for support. My whole world came crashing down around me, I was lost and I had no idea what to do.

I walked into the kitchen where my mum was cooking breakfast. I looked at her and suddenly the look she had had on her face when I was discussing which job I would take made sense: it was a look of wisdom. It was also her struggle to resist her motherly instinct to protect me but she had to let me be a man. She knew I was being naïve because it was unlikely I would get all three jobs but she didn't want to burst my enthusiasm. I learnt a valuable lesson that day, and I will always be grateful to my mother for letting me learn it.

'Are you all right?' she asked softly.

My bottom lip began to quiver as I mumbled, I didn't get the Safeway's job.'

'Oh, I'm sorry darling.'

She put her arms out and I eagerly accepted the invitation and hugged her as tightly as I could. For those few moments I reverted back to the ten year old boy who longed for his mother's embrace. In her arms I felt safe. I was so scared to let her go because that was the moment I realised I was not as prepared for the world as I thought.

My Mother and I, June 2012

Lightning Source UK Ltd.
Milton Keynes UK
UKOW041342240912

199546UK00001B/6/P

9 781781 485644